What People Are Saying About Regina DuBose

"Regina is a great businesswoman who responsibly handles her customers and friends with respect, making their needs a priority. I have utilized her services many times, for company picnics, church celebrations, and birthday gatherings. She has provided a variety of personalized, small gift items, including t-shirts, hats, water bottles, and balloon decorations, all of which have received extremely high compliments in regards to quality work and materials.

I have also witnessed Regina overcome many obstacles along her journey. She has dealt with periods without transportation, financial challenges, and family difficulties, yet her faith in God's Word and plan for her life have pushed to persevere through it all.

Regina's consistency, compassion and dedication are not only demonstrated in her business, but also in family. As a single parent, she supported her daughter through college and graduate school, while taking care of her mother in her final days. She is a true inspiration.

God has His hand on Regina's life and that she is obedient and faithful to his Word.

I love my Sister in Christ and I am excited to see where God takes her in the next level on her journey."

—**Jackie Jones**, *Member, Unity Baptist Church*

"Regina DuBose, owner of The Alexis Company, has been doing t-shirts for my company for many years. She was located on Gratiot Avenue in the Eastern Market area of Detroit, Michigan. Her company was always professional, no matter how small or large your order.

My company re-connected with her again when I was doing plays with Ms. Shirley Rayford, her church member. So, The Alexis Company started doing t-shirts for my skating parties and all my plays.

Great work and GREAT memories."

—**Shawn P. Williams,** *Shawn P. Entertainment*

"I met Regina over 15 years ago. She has always been a committed businesswoman. She created some apparel for my business and did a great job. Regina is a top-notch business professional. She takes time to motivate other people in business. Being in business for 35 years, she has to be doing something right!"

—**Fred D. Gordon,** *Owner, FDG Computer Services, LLC*

"I had the pleasure of meeting Sister Regina DuBose in 2003 as our church, New Prospect Missionary Baptist Church, was preparing to participate in the Susan G. Komen Race for the Cure. That year, we had a little over 300 race participants.

Sister Regina pushed out the orders for not just t-shirts, but matching gold hats as well. Our team lit up Woodward Avenue in those gold shirts and hats. Everyone, from the TV commentators, Race Planning Committee, and other race participants, commented on New Prospect's *Sea of Gold* shirts! That was the beginning of a soon-to-be 20-year relationship between New Prospect Missionary Baptist Church and Alexis Novelty and Gifts.

Sister Regina is an extraordinary entrepreneur and business-woman, and a fine woman of God who lovingly cares for others. Sister Regina, I say *bravo* to you; job well done! Knowing you and working with you have been a true blessing for me! Thank you for blessing New Prospect by sharing your God-given talents and gifts! Congratulations on the success of your business and celebration of 35 years! And added congratulations on your success as a published author. May God continue to bless you, as you bless others."

—**Jeanette Hall Girty**, *Member, New Prospect Missionary Baptist Church*

"I have had the pleasure of working with Ms. Regina DuBose and The Alexis Company for three of my family reunions from 2010 to 2016. Ms. DuBose's services have been superb. The quality of t-shirts, the lettering, and the pricing are second to none."

—**Tasha Squires**, *Certified Meeting Planner*

"I met Regina DuBose through Beverly Williams, who is the director of the Seniors Program at Adams Butzel Recreation Center.

Ms. Regina started doing t-shirts for our Seniors Program about seven or eight years ago. During that time, she was always a reliable vendor, getting our merchandise to us in a timely manner.

Thank you, Ms. Regina, for your professionalism. I look forward to continuing to doing business with The Alexis Company. Because of your kind and Christian way, I say that is the key to keeping customers and having a successful business."

—**Ms. Delora Acker**, *Merchandising Assoc., Butzel Adams Rec. Center*

"I began doing business in the late '90s with Regina when The Alexis Company was located on Gratiot Avenue, near downtown Detroit. As a professional Mary Kay Beauty Consultant since 1982, I purchased gift baskets to merchandise my products for various holidays.

In addition, Regina rendered outstanding services for our family reunion when she printed and delivered t-shirts ahead of schedule. Even though she was not driving at the time, appointments were always kept by way of the bus. That speaks volumes in being a 'committed and determined' businesswoman!

As true women of God, we stand in the combined choirs of Unity Baptist Church, and we also grew up in the same neighborhood. I am truly grateful that our paths crossed, and it's a blessing we have become great friends."

—Jacqueline Harvard-Harris, *Mary Kay Consultant*

"Regina DuBose, a successful, long-time Detroit entrepreneur, tells us her secret formula for starting and keeping a thriving business. DuBose takes us through a series of crucial steps that teach us how to master the entrepreneurial spirit. She shares her personal story to demonstrate how to overcome the challenges of being a small business owner with passion and zeal. DuBose never says never, and her success is a testament to that motto.

DuBose becomes the reader's own personal mentor in the small business world. From various topics such as skill development, marketing, financial acumen, emotional development, and business relationships, she helps you become the small business owner you have always dreamed of being.

DuBose encourages you to take a chance and learn about your potential as an entrepreneur. And after you create your business, you will learn how to develop the tools to make it last!"

—**Mrs. Ann Edwards**, *First Impressions Day Care*

"I must say, I really enjoyed reading your manuscript. I have to add that it gave me such a thrill to read so much detail and great memory of your journey.

I see where your book will help a lot of people enjoy the purpose of business, and the enlightenment of getting to know others. I also see where your beginning has no end.

And you have really taken my thought process to another level. I thank you."

—**Darnell Glover**, *Salon On The Park*

"This book was fabulous. You really stated all the details and tips on how to succeed in running your own business. Examples include how to treat customers with respect and listening to their concerns. I also went to Wayne State. And my dad also taught me what you stated: word of mouth is very important to growing. I wish you all the success, and I know the book will be on the top of the list on Amazon!"

—**Judy Epstein**, *National Dry Goods*

"This book should be in every female's collection of inspiring books. Regina's book is a collection of empowering business and leadership advice. She is an incredible woman with an incredible story. I have had the pleasure of knowing Regina for 10+ years. I am writing this review in memory of my late father, Dominic Ciaravino, who encouraged her to pursue and start her own screen-printing business. Today, my brother and I continue to honor our father's legacy, encouraging and teaching others to start their own screen-printing business.

I love how Regina perfectly captures how to turn every obstacle in her life into a positive experience and chase your dream. Her determination to learn and succeed is an example that if we want anything badly enough, we can achieve it.

Pursue your passions and make your lives more meaningful like Regina DuBose has. She is truly the definition of a business leader and it shows. Regina has 'gone the extra mile' and has written a great book that blends business, sales, marketing, insight, experience, spirituality, giving back to the community and more… It is truly a great read!"

—**Sandy Riddell**, *Screen Tek Imaging Solutions*

"I was introduced to Mrs. Regina DuBose by her daughter, Dr. Sequina DuBose of Charlotte, NC. I mentioned to her that I needed someone to print my family reunion's t-shirts, and she said, 'Call my mother, that is her business.'

We met by phone in 2019 and her company printed my family reunion with t-shirts (White Family Reunion, 22nd Year Anniversary, in Madeira Beach, Florida). She did an excellent job and was such a joy to work with.

Subsequently, The Alexis Company became the print company for the Afro-American Historical and Genealogical Society, Inc., Charlotte Chapter (AAHGS) for our t-shirts and other promotional materials.

Mrs. DuBose's knowledge base and wisdom, as a Christian woman and a successful entrepreneur, have been an invaluable blessing me. I am so excited for her, and cannot wait to read her books!"

—**Renee Y. Jones**, MBA — President, AAHGS, Charlotte, NC

PERPETUATING
WEALTH

Secrets to Longevity
in Small Business

Strategies From an Entrepreneur
After 35 Years of Success
at
The Alexis Company

Regina DuBose

ATKINS & GREENSPAN PUBLISHING

For information about this title or to order other books and/or
electronic media, contact the publisher:

Atkins & Greenspan Publishing
TwoSistersWriting.com
18530 Mack Avenue, Suite 166
Grosse Pointe Farms, MI 48236

ISBN 978-1-945875-84-7 (Hardcover)
ISBN 978-1-945875-83-0 (Paperback)
ISBN 978-1-945875-85-4 (eBook)

Printed in the United States of America

Cover and Interior design: Ivory Coast Media and Van-garde Imagery, Inc.

Author Photo: Anita Bonnie Harrell

All photographs used with permission. All uncredited photographs
courtesy of The Alexis Company Collection.

Dedication

To my daughter, Sequina Bianca DuBose, who motivated me throughout this journey.

To my customers, who support our existence.

And to my first employer, Thompson & Edwards, CPAs who taught me everything I know about the entrepreneurial experience.

Contents

Photo Collection – The Alexis Company
1986–2021

WE HAVE INCLUDED SOME pictures which document the path of our accomplishments during the entrepreneurial journey.

My dream begins with The Alexis Company, also known as Alexis Novelty & Gifts Company, where our motto is "Where the FUN Begins…"

We are Detroit's exciting novelty, party supply, souvenir, and tee shirt business with a proven track record of success. We are thankful for our customers, friends, supporters, and patrons!

So, enjoy the photos which document our history, progress, community involvement, and achievements. Serving our customers in the spirit of excellence has been our goal throughout the journey.

"Where The Fun Begins..."™

Anniversary
35th Celebration 2021
www.thealexiscompany.com
Since 1986

PREFACE

BEHIND THE SCENES, I think my mother was a great psychologist. When she died, I wrote a poem about her titled, "The Great Producer." She used to say, "You never hear me bragging on my children, because I don't know what they're doing when I'm not around!" She said it so often that when she and my dad were out, my brothers and I knew how to behave. We did not want to disappoint them. We had a desire to make them proud. Especially me, I guess because I was the only girl in the family.

My full name is Regina Alexis DuBose, and I was born in 1957 to Samuel Matthew and Rosie Lee Hinkle. I was raised on the west side in Detroit, Michigan with my four brothers: Samuel Jr., Ronnie, William, and James. Our family stood out because my youngest brother, James, was born handicapped. My mother was given the Thalidomide drug during her last pregnancy.

The neighborhood was filled with Polish and Black American families who were learning, working, and playing together in a viable community where goods and services were within walking distance. We had an active block club where the parents were chaperones and sponsors for activities and trips. It was fun growing up and I spent time trying to keep up with the boys. The riot in Detroit occurred during the summer of 1967. The next year, our family started attending church regularly.

I attended Hanneman Elementary School and was the Spelling Bee Champion for two consecutive years. My sixth-grade teacher, Mrs. Crews, always said, "You are so smart." When I got to Munger Junior High, it was in the eighth grade that my homeroom teacher, Mr. Robert Hague, mentioned that Cass Technical High School was admitting ninth graders and encouraged me to enroll.

"You have good grades," he said. "Do you want to go?"

And I distinctly remember saying, "Yes, because I want to see if I am as smart as my oldest brother, Junior." Samuel Jr. was already a student at that prestigious public high school, and was the leader of the family when our parents were working or shopping. He certainly was a taskmaster and made sure that our household chores were done by the time they returned home. We often played "tag team wrestling" in their absence. Yet, somehow we could always hear the car door slam just before they entered the home and saw us sitting in an orderly fashion. We thought we were pulling their legs.

It was 1971 when I enrolled in high school. I had to catch the bus because it was a distance from my neighborhood. The place was this huge factory-looking building with seven floors—nothing like I had ever seen before in education. The new ninth-grade students came from various neighborhoods throughout the city. All races, different backgrounds, a mixture of socioeconomic statuses, and variance in personality dynamics. The one seemingly common denominator was that we were all high achievers and go-getters who were primed for greatness and success. That was so appealing to me. As far as I know, I was the only one from my neighborhood who was a bright, new ninth-grader. I felt special.

One day while traveling home on a crowded bus, the students were being pushy, trying to get on and off the bus. This guy was standing in the aisle, and others were saying to him, "Excuse me! Let me get by!" and, "Hey, move, please. This is my stop."

When I needed to politely pass him, he looked me in the eyes and said, "I guess you want to be excused, too!"

My response was, "Yes."

As he let me pass, I thought, "Now that's the kind of guy I'd like to marry. He's a gentleman." From that point on, when school was dismissed, I would always hope or look to see if he was riding the same bus as me. This young man gave me the giggles.

On Valentine's Day in 1972, Sequoia DuBose asked me to be his girlfriend and we courted throughout high school. Also, later that year, I got my first job as a clerk-typist at Thompson & Edwards, CPAs, located in the Penobscot Building downtown Detroit.

I had a great schedule which allowed me to leave school by noon to go to work. There I learned so much about business, such as: information about the big eight accounting firms; how to write a check and manage a bank account; the best ways to interact with clients; the different business entities; the meaning of "fiscal year-end"; telephone etiquette; bookkeeping; organizing financial statements; and preparing and filing income taxes.

I was responsible for making the coffee, copying returns, and handling the mail, all while learning the professional world of a small business. I was the youngest employee at the firm and the only African American. Upon my hiring, my father gave his approval only after he visited the office to meet everyone. I worked there from 1972 until 1978. The firm paid for my wedding night at the Renaissance Center downtown Detroit.

My place of employment was the environment that fueled the fire within me to reach for the stars of excellence in everything that I pursued. I got to see life from a different perspective. I was respected and soon had a key to the office. I was on the team. They saw my potential and provided the avenue and tools for me to grow. My introduction to the world of business was enlightened as a direct result of working at a young age. However, I changed my major from business to psychology in college after re-dedicating my life to God. I decided instead to be a guidance counselor.

My high school sweetheart and I got married in 1978, and upon finishing college at Wayne State University in 1980, we relocated to New York City. He received the Thurgood Marshall Scholarship to attend New York Law School, while I was finishing my Masters in Guidance and Counseling. I was pregnant at the time and our daughter was born on the first day of law school. Surprised that our new baby was a girl, I had not thought about the name. However, he had already come up with her name, "Sequina," combining both of our names.

Eventually, I started working as a guidance counselor at a Jewish agency in lower Manhattan. We had a lot of "firsts" in our relationship over the years, grew closer, faced challenges, traveled to Europe, and knew that life was better when two people work, struggle, and love together. However, our marriage took a turn for the worse and we wound up getting a divorce.

During the summer of 1984, an old colleague, Hamel, who worked in New York, telephoned and said he had quit his job and was working the Michael Jackson Thriller Tour!

"You quit your job as a counselor?" I asked. "Really?"

"Yes," he said, and asked me to come to the Pontiac Silverdome where the performance was being held to see their operation. After the concert, as people were walking to their vehicles, his group shouted "Michael Jackson gloves, five dollars, five dollars!" They had a bunch of white, glittered gloves similar to the one that the King of Pop wore, and people went crazy buying these gloves.

I was simply amazed, because all this commotion was happening outside, at night, in the parking lot. His friend, Jeffrey, who was from Philadelphia, was the main leader, and we exchanged telephone numbers.

"Regina," Jeffrey said, "let me know of future events in the Detroit area if you want to make some extra money."

"Okay," I said, having already shared with Hamel on the phone that my marriage was rocky and wavering and I could use some "extra money." But I was fascinated by this way of making money.

By October 1984, the "Roar of 1984" was in full swing and the Detroit Tigers were in the World Series. It was getting close to the last two games and the Tigers were in the lead. Jeffrey called and asked if I would go down to the stadium, stand on a corner, and sell "t-shirts." Mind you, I had a degree, a job, and a baby. I was separated from my husband and had neither the knowledge nor any reputation of "standing on the corner" to sell anything in the City of Detroit. Still, I said, "I'll give it a try." Well, my fear suddenly went to fervor, because the Tigers won that night and fans bought all the shirts that Jeffrey had shipped.

After the Tigers went on to win the Championship, Jeffrey called to say, "I'm flying into Detroit to work tomorrow. Can you work the parade?"

"What?" I exclaimed. "The Parade? No, I have to go to my job." I thought, *What a guy. He is something else!* Yet, he did pay me 25 percent from my sales. This was a new, unknown highway that I was being asked to travel. The idea of making money and flying around the country, while working concerts and special events, was unfamiliar.

"What are you doing with your money?" I asked him.

"Mutual funds," he always replied.

I was curious and impressed with this process. It was new, different, and strange, yet interesting.

But time and chance happen to all of us. So, Jeffrey went out on the limb to contact me one more time in November of 1984. It was to sell for the Prince Purple Rain Tour. The recording artist was opening his tour in Detroit due to the loyal fan base over the years. He planned to perform seven concert nights. Jeffrey came to town with a variety of Prince paraphernalia that we could possibly sell. We settled on the "light up-rose," because I insisted that we would not get into any trouble, given that it was a neutral product and did not have Prince's name on it. We secured two vendors' licenses and permits. The album had a bunch of flowers and roses printed on it. And to top it off, the recording artist dropped flowers from the ceiling on the first song; he also gave roses to fans seated on the front rows midway during the concert.

Our sales went straight to the roof at four dollars each! I was bitten by the bug of the entrepreneur! This indeed was an exciting, fun, new, way for generating income. I was flabbergasted!

From that moment on, our crew followed Prince's Purple Rain Tour every weekend, making money by selling these light-up roses, as concert-goers were walking through the parking lot to their cars.

The extra funds enabled me to purchase a new Ford Escort. On many occasions, I returned home from these trips in the wee hours of the morning on Mondays, just in the nick of time to make it to my place of employment!

In January of 1985, I asked my father to sponsor a weekend trip to California, where the San Francisco Forty-Niners were playing the Miami Dolphins in the Super Bowl. I felt I could use my new "sales experience" and was ready for a major football championship.

When I made it from the airport to Stanford Stadium, on the campus of Stanford University, carrying 300 pennants inside my duffle bag, tailgate parties were happening everywhere I turned. The people were friendly—celebrating, offering me food and beverages—while purchasing the pennants. I walked around the grounds, selling off and on throughout the game, and when the Forty-Niners won, everybody was partying and celebrating! It was a phenomenal sight to experience!

Interestingly, of all the large vendor spots, I saw only one African American man who was running a stand. His name was Howard, a vendor from New Haven, Connecticut. He raved about his travels in this field of working special events, carnivals, and major sports championships. Before we exchanged telephone numbers, I asked him, "Which company sells these licensed t-shirts and merchandise?"

But my request was ignored with a smile and a puzzled look. He couldn't believe that some small, African American woman from Detroit, Michigan was out there, "selling pennants by herself, for herself." He was shocked! However, I knew that something more awaited my discovery in this realm of business. So I just smiled and held my peace.

It was getting late, and the people were heading downtown for late into-the-night festivities. I realized that my returning flight to Detroit was early in the morning, so I did some final sales and began to pack my bag. However, I noticed the workers throwing away empty boxes as they were breaking down the huge vending stands. When they finally drove off in their trucks, I went straight to the rubbish area and tore off the different labels from the boxes of various suppliers. I was thinking about the possibility of vending at future sporting events, and being in the position to contact them directly for officially licensed merchandise.

When I returned to Detroit, my brother Ronnie had an idea to continue selling the light-up roses in lounges, clubs, and cabarets, as well as for birthday parties. This was timely, because the Prince Tour was traveling to the west coast in the USA, too far from our jobs, and too expensive for weekend travel. So on Friday and Saturday nights, we continued to make money locally. Finally, one night a lady asked if she could purchase some light-up roses at a wholesale price so that she herself could sell them at a party. After saying, "Yes," I started thinking about owning and running a store. The quest was on to find a great location and set up an establishment for the general public.

On March 16, 1986, we opened our store, The Alexis Company, at 1410 Gratiot Avenue in Detroit, Michigan, in the 48207 zip code. It was located in the Eastern Market Area. I had two people who did everything to make it happen: from painting the walls, to mopping the floors, to interacting with new customers, and to picking up equipment. My brother Ronnie and my nephew Samuel III were the main support system in this new venture of selling to consumers on a larger scale. The company grew tremendously and we cultivated our trademark logo, which has been our brand. We adopted our motto/slogan: "Where the Fun Begins…" and we have provided a host of exciting novelties, party supplies, souvenirs, and t-shirts to our customers.

The Alexis Company, also known as The Alexis Novelty & Gifts Company, has served thousands of customers in the Metropolitan Detroit region and across the nation for more than 35 years.

In *Perpetuating Wealth*, I'm sharing my secrets for longevity in small business success while encouraging others to pursue their entrepreneurial dreams.

Anniversary
35th Celebration 2021
www.thealexiscompany.com
Since 1986

"Where The Fun Begins..." ™

Novelty * Balloons * Decorations * Gifts * Souvenirs * Caps
Sportswear * Silk Screen * Embroidery * Fundraising
Party Supplies * Union Printing

410-303-1726
www.thealexiscompany.com

A Proven Track Record for Over 35 Years!
Since 1986

Introduction

AFTER YOU START YOUR own business, wouldn't it be great if someone provided you with the necessary tools to help you stay in business? Statistically, nine out of 10 businesses fail within the first five years, as mentioned in *CASHFLOW Quadrant: Rich Dad's Guide to Financial Freedom* by Robert Kiyosaki and Sharon Lechter, CPA[1]. That means, 99 out of 100 small companies go out of business during the first decade. When you consider those numbers, that is huge.

Although many people may start an enterprise, unfortunately most fail at operating and maintaining a small business. Sometimes it is because they get on the wrong track, and never readjust to get back on the right track. If this happens too early in the entrepreneurial game, it can be a devastating blow, both financially and emotionally.

I took the opportunity to visit the IRS Small Business and Tax Center internet page, and saw categories that can help an individual who ventures into the small business arena. This includes information on Starting a Business, Operating a Business, and Closing a Business. You can find facts on Self Employment, Independent Contractors, and Business Taxes. Another section helps you determine your Business Structure, Recordkeeping, and Business Tax

Credits. A number of key factors are presented in the Forms and Publications that are specifically geared for Small Business ventures. However, I did not find any section on "How to Stay in Business," after you have taken such a daring step to control your own destiny and financial well-being.

The rewards from owning, managing, and building your own business are so vast. In fact, too many exist to mention here, but if you never learn how to **stay in business,** you will never be able to reap the benefits from having your ideas grow into a viable enterprise. So, when does that happen? What are the signs? The moment you recognize that your business stands out and shines.

We have an outstanding history of small business success at The Alexis Company and Alexis Novelty & Gifts Company. It has been remarkable. Now—as of October 2021—we're celebrating our 35th year of servicing our customers by presenting this guidebook that shows how to stay in business over time.

This book presents key elements that we pulled from our resources, extensive background, vibrant history, and unique experience of serving our customers and the general public.

It has not been a hard journey, and yet it has not been any easy task, either. It takes stamina and resilience to run a successful small business. Those two factors are a must! That's it in a nutshell. Remember that one fact as you read on and become successful at what you do, while serving others.

Looking back, I can recall so many disappointing moments where the final decision had to be made: "Do or die. Continue or give up. Stop or go forward." In most cases, a simple redirection would come into my view to force some heightened growth and development. And when some of those hard times led to a reduction in profit margin, I literally had to re-evaluate my plans, re-think my goals, and ask myself, "Why am I doing this? Where is the money going? What's happening right now that makes sense?"

But really. It doesn't take that much. I believe that a little effort can go a long way. So, I have selected some basic steps—My Business Secrets—that are easy for you to follow and review from time to time, and that can help you maintain a thriving business: one that is financially rewarding, wholesome, and productive, all while helping to fulfill your dreams. The information that I will share with you can assist in navigating your business so that you can flourish and grow despite the changing economy, political environment, and various consumer trends that may impact your goals. The world of an entrepreneur is a place where all possibilities exist. Now go forward and seize the moment!

Regina Alexis DuBose
President

Chapter 1

GO THE EXTRA MILE

READY? GET SET. LET'S go!

Whether you're starting a new business venture, or looking for ways to enhance an old one, I must challenge you to consider the following questions as we begin this journey together. Yes, it's our aim to discuss and show you my secrets to stay in small business. First, you must ask yourself: How do I plan to stay in business? Why am I really in business? What do I actually do in my business? Who is really going to benefit from my business? When will I know that my business is a real benefit to me and to others? Where is my business going? Where is it right now? Where have I been with this business? What meaning does this business have for me personally? Remember to ask yourself these questions as you ponder your pursuits in business.

I'm a long-distance runner. I can run for long distances and not get tired. That is what it means to **go the extra mile**. To stay in a small business, you have to be able to run long distances, even when you have only a short amount of time. You may have just enough time to make an impression, or a brief moment to surprise your customer, or a quick second to say, "I really do appreciate your business." It is so important to go beyond the immediate call of duty. You need ongoing strength, endurance, and intuition to progress.

Over the years, we have learned to handle each customer's individual request as if it were the only sale for that entire day. In fact, that one sale just might be the one that pays the monthly rent. This is the key to repeat business and a long list of satisfied customers. Special attention goes a long way.

Many good businesses fail and go out of business because the owners/managers rarely step inside the shoes of the actual customer and ask:

1) Did I do my very best to make sure the customer was completely satisfied?

2) Did I give them the best price for the product that was purchased?

3) Is there anything I could have done differently that would have led to a better outcome?

Repeat business is the glue to stay in business. When you go the extra mile, you apply pressure to the bottle that will continue to squeeze out more and more glue.

Get used to the fact that customers talk. Whether you realize it or not, they talk regularly to one another. Sometimes, they even spill the beans about a product or service, right in your presence. They talk to other customers at home, on the telephone, on their jobs, and at the movie theater. Customers talk to themselves in their thoughts (about the experience with you and your business). And they talk to people who are potential customers. All this talking about you and your business is summed up in the catch-all phrase: "word of mouth." It eventually gets around to those who matter the most—possible referrals to your company and everyone else who will decide to patronize and support your small business.

The extra things that you do, intentionally and unintentionally, actually create a lot of talking—you can call it "good noise"—about how well you function and handle your business. Your professionalism is measured. How you perform in meeting deadlines might be evaluated. And people will analyze your ability to speak with authority in an impromptu setting. This inevitably leads to longevity in business.

"The extra mile mentality" inspires people to have positive conversations about you, your attitude, and your approach to business—all the while helping you to stay in business. And in fact, you may even surprise yourself as to how far you will go to guarantee customer satisfaction. In many cases, over the years, I have often surpassed the finish line, grabbed the trophy and the ribbon, and finally sat down (to breathe). Here are some examples of "the extra mile mentality" that helped us along the way to remain a viable, small business in the community.

- I once drove 45 miles to deliver birthday balloons to the relative of a customer who was staying in a drug rehabilitation center in the suburbs.

- One evening, a customer came into my store to pick up her order right at closing time. When she walked back to her vehicle, the tire was flat. I reopened the store and called AAA road service and waited for them to arrive before ending my day. They arrived two hours past my closing time.

- At the last minute, on the day of a family reunion event, a customer needed "extra t-shirts." We took the shirts directly to the cookout site early the next morning, way before everyone else arrived.

- Over the years, we have been fortunate enough to donate many of our products to support the needs and fundraisers that were given by many nonprofit organizations, local groups, schools, and churches.

Going the extra mile certainly pays off in the long run. Customers generally tend to like that special attention, and will definitely remember **You,** before they select another option, which is often your competition. When you guarantee customer satisfaction, you'll stay in business longer, and smile all the way to the bank!

Chapter 2

Do What Others Are Not Going To Do

LET'S FACE IT. OTHER businesses, the competition, and the guy who has been claiming the market in your town for the past 50 years, are not going to do what you do. The fact of the matter is, they don't have to. In most cases, they have already paid their own dues, changed the rules, earned their share of the market, or simply been at the right place at the right time in history.

To develop a niche—that special thing that distinguishes your business from the next person and keeps your cash register ringing—takes: trial and error, practice, practice, practice; brainstorming; and trying new ideas to improve the quality of your business output. To stay focused, despite the showboating you may notice from the competition, it is very important and requires stamina to "see" and "hear," but not be affected by their progress. Don't let what other businesses are doing distract you from your own objectives.

Learn to do what others are not willing to do. Sometimes, it may take too much money for other businesses to see the benefit in your approach. That may be a good thing. And what's good for your business may be terrible for another company. Take advantage of being the small guy or new kid on the block.

Take the time to visit the locations of other businesses and check out how they operate. It is very helpful to experience a direct competitor, as well as other businesses who are completely different from your operation. This wise experiment can be quite revealing and insightful, showing you what others are not willing or capable of doing. I often visit other businesses to observe how their employees function, to witness how they treat their customers, and to test their atmosphere for generating sales. This also gives you the opportunity to check out their product line and merchandise classification. You may find that they are not a big threat or hindrance to your course of action.

Learn what you can do differently to get your piece of the "market action" that other companies may have overlooked, or simply do not promote. For instance, consider a balloon service that delivers and handles orders that are picked up by the customers. We have had great progress with our delivery system over the past 35 years, delivering our products to customers' homes, office buildings, construction work sites, hospitals, private clubs, affluent residential areas, various schools, and college campuses.

Customers with busy schedules appreciate this wonderful convenience. It has earned us many "brownie points" with our customers for our professionalism and timely service. We realized that it was essential to implement a customized delivery system to meet our patrons' needs, so that we could stand out from others, doing what they were not going to do. This has helped us stay in business, month after month, year after year. Our service is one that people really value and use consistently.

No matter what they tell you, it pays to develop your own formula for winning. Something you can believe in and adhere to in your quest to stay in business. Choose a personal philosophy that really matters to you, despite what other people think, say, feel, or do. Decide on a formula that you can practice and fully implement within the structure of your business environment. One that becomes real, and is respected by your staff members, will go a long way. They will adhere to the mantra as they rely on each other and establish a bond.

My formula came to me in our 16th year (Yes, it took that long!) of business, while we were promoting a Sweet Sixteen Outdoor Party to thank the community for their support over the years. This was in 2002; I had sent a press release to Ms. Betty DeRamus, formerly of *The Detroit Free Press* and *The Detroit News*, and she phoned for more information about how we were celebrating our 16th Business Anniversary.

"What has been your formula for success?" Ms. DeRamus asked.

"Prayer, Patience, Planning, and Passion," I answered. Then as I thought about my entrepreneurial journey up to that point, I realized what has been significantly important to help us sustain the business. You know what I did next? Immediately after my conversation with her, I grabbed a pencil and wrote the "4 P's" while it was fresh in my head. And I meditated on how each principle had been an integral part of staying in business and a part of our continued progress. Since that time, our formula has not changed. It is still Prayer, Patience, Planning, and Passion!

I love what I do and I do what I love! Sometimes it feels like magic in the air! Especially now, since we have a proven track record over a significant period of time. So many years have passed. I am thankful to God for my joy.

To stay in business, you must figure out a way to work *on* your business, instead of just working *in* our business. Honestly speaking, it took me a few years to figure this one out. I spent many days focusing on how to keep the ball rolling. Keeping my customers satisfied, the cash register ringing, paying my staff well, maintaining the store's atmosphere, and dealing with the monthly bills. This was a constant juggling act.

You need to know the distinct difference between working "on" your business versus "in" your business.

Working "on" your business involves taking the time to develop new plans or strategies, sometimes brainstorming with staff for new ideas, and coming up with ways to improve product or service output. It includes designing the business logo or motto, etcetera. Basically, it involves doing things to improve the overall future outlook, projections, and goals of the small business. You may need to spend some time re-examining sections of your business plan to evaluate your approach to meeting your desired objectives. Ask yourself: "Are we on schedule? Are we doing the right things for this moment in time? What can we do better?" Ask these questions during fun, explorative problem-solving sessions that improve your overall output or bottom line, while moving your business forward.

Working "in" your business means handling the day-to-day operations and functions that generate revenue and ongoing sales. This is the lifeblood of being in business. And to stay in business, someone has to do it. Either you or the people you hire must know how to write up new customer orders, handle questions from customers, keep the floors clean, manage the daily flow of telephone requests, and handle the day-to-day activities, which always seem to vary.

So it is very important to recognize how you will function, given the demands of your business and the need to focus on continued growth and management. In short, working on your business produces *continued effective growth*. And working in your business produces *continued effective management*. You need to do both to stay in business. Actually, you must learn to "see the forest" and the individual "trees" simultaneously. This will allow you to generate a broad and narrow perspective of your small business, and help you stay focused on profit margins, growth, research, development, and expansion into new markets.

People often ask me, "Do customers complain?" And the answer is, "Yes, of course, they do." And how you handle their concerns affects whether or not you will continue to stay in business. It is hard to try and please every customer. Some people are difficult to satisfy, but if you give it your best shot, you will never lose. Explanations for complaints should be given with authority, handled with dignity, and processed thoroughly to resolve differences. It's best to avoid "catch-all phrases," easy excuses, poorly trained employees, and verbal abuse. People can be sensitive and extremely disappointed when their concerns are not addressed. They can become more distraught when they are not considered important enough to work out an amenable solution.

You will find that other businesses, like the guy I spoke about at the beginning of this chapter who's been cornering the market for the past 50 years, may be able to skirt over a problem. But most small businesses cannot afford the luxury of ignoring the average customer's complaint. I suggest that you think it through, act quickly, and resolve the matter so that everyone wins. The longer you wait, the more convoluted the message can become and stir up ill feelings. Mixed messages create a lot of conflict, which can destroy the best of all intentions. Stay ahead of the game by settling those differences that a customer may present in a prompt, orderly fashion.

Chapter 3

Know Your
Proficiency Level

Small business owners and managers are often all over the place. Many do not know what they are doing, and most cannot define their own existence. Sometimes the need to make a dollar outweighs the need to firm up your ideas and become proficient in a specific area. Listen, you don't have to be the great master or an expert, but it's imperative to maintain a good working knowledge of the purpose and mission of your business. Maintain a good understanding of your status.

A "Jack of All Trades" has his place in society. However, it's better to be a small business owner who has a specialty and who stays around for a long time. Therefore, it's so important to know your proficiency level. In other words, what's good about your business, and what's not so good? Ask yourself some good questions that encourage you to focus on what things your company does well. Once you find the answers, begin to build on that kind of momentum and try to become an expert in that particular area.

Once your performance level increases, you will realize and obtain more business experiences that will heighten your level of expertise, increase your specialization, and expand your classification. That's what happened in my business. I was very surprised when it occurred—and very, very happy.

We started out as a small novelty company in 1986 with *one* little item: "the light-up rose." This is still my favorite product! It's an artificial, battery-operated, 15-inch silk rose that lights up. It comes in purple, red, or pink. We must have sold thousands of these purple roses during The Purple Rain Tour with the famous recording artist, Prince, who died in 2018. The tour began in November 1984 with several performance nights in Detroit, Michigan, and concluded during the summer of 1985.

After that tour ended, my brother suggested that we continue to sell the roses at local night clubs, lounges, cabarets, and birthday celebrations. This shift led us to make money by attending local parties, galas, and even the big Valentine's Day Dance. Sponsored by the late, great Detroit Mayor Coleman A. Young, it was held in the Riverfront Ballroom of Cobo Hall, which was a major venue at that time.

Growth can catch you by surprise. Here's what I mean. One evening, a lady asked if she could buy the roses "wholesale" from us and sell them at her own party, rather than having us come to her big bash. Immediately, the light bulb in my head lit up and I thought, *Bingo! Now that would be great! We can sell the roses to more people at the wholesale price, and make a whole lot of money!*

Then I told my brother, "We need a store!" So I started looking for a place to move all those boxes of roses that were stored in our parents' basement. The quest was on to begin to sell at a whole new level. All because one simple question had ignited a force within us to reach more people.

After driving around the City of Detroit, I came across an empty building located on Gratiot Avenue near downtown in the bustling Eastern Market neighborhood. It's home to the sprawling and historic farmers market and surrounding shops and restaurants that draw huge crowds on the weekends. In fact, as a child, I accompanied my parents on Saturday mornings as they shopped amongst vendors, fruit and vegetable stands, flowers and plants, and a popular meat market. This nostalgic connection to the area, plus my knowledge of the tens of thousands of people who shopped there every weekend, made this an ideal location. Another plus? At the time in 1986, no other novelty/t-shirt company was located in the surrounding area.

The building was the former home of Detroit Knitting Mills during the 1970's. A sign in the window said, "For Rent." I called the owner, made the inquiry, and the rest is history.

We opened our first store location on March 16, 1986, at 1410 Gratiot Avenue, Detroit, Michigan 48207. It was monumental. A definite game-changer in our world as new entrepreneurs!

Location, location, location is definitely the main ingredient for small business success. The Eastern Market Area is one of the best locations in the City of Detroit. Listed on the National Register of Historic Places, it's a thriving hub of artists, vendors, small business owners, and of course, the vast farmers market. It also has a direct connection to city services and plans for long term development. It has a special culture amongst the residents, patrons, and supporters of the area. Everyone embraces the unique environment of the **Eastern Market and National Register of Historic Places.**

Of course, I knew that we could not survive with just one product to maintain a viable business, so I started to investigate the novelty field. I found only one major novelty business in the entire city, which seemed to have everything from roses, to whistles, to balloons, and a variety of party supplies. So, I began to make weekly purchases from that company, little by little, adding new novelty merchandise to my small business. The frequency of my visits, and my weekly purchases, which usually amounted to $100 or more, prompted the owner to ask me on several occasions: "So, what are you doing?"

Of course, I never said, "I'm the new novelty kid on the block, who's adding merchandise to my store." Instead, I would respond, "Oh, I'm working on a few parties and events."

But that is exactly what was going on. I was adding his merchandise to build up my store's inventory, marking the prices just a wee bit higher, only to see a small profit. One day I asked him, "Where do you get your merchandise?"

He gave no response—only a look! A strange, kind of weird, sarcastic look with one eyebrow raised! It said: "I wonder what she's really up to?" I could tell that more questions were roaming through his mind.

Then, I noticed that *no other similar business or novelty company* owned by an African American (male or female) existed in the entire city. No such business was operating in the local neighborhoods—nothing at the shopping centers or the malls, nor was any business of this type situated downtown in the heart of the city. So, I started going to the Main Branch of the Detroit Public Library to investigate and delve into the Novelty business. I was fascinated by this new adventure, and wanted to learn more, given the non-existence of this industry in our city, though it really did exist elsewhere. I had found this brave, new world to explore and possibly conquer. I was motivated, indeed!

After finding a comfortable seat in the Business Section of the library, I spent several weeks investigating and learning about "novelty suppliers, distributors, manufacturers, wholesalers, and retail operators." These places were located in various cities throughout the nation. They provided these funny products, the kinds of items you would rarely see in the average toy store, yet were niceties that seemed to just "make your day."

My days and weeks of learning at the library took many long hours and a huge dose of consistency. This was years before the instant, information magic of the internet. I simply enjoyed the "hands on" approach to learning, while experiencing the quiet atmosphere and the human interaction at the public library. Librarians are great research professionals.

Meanwhile, after decades of operating in the City of Detroit, my long-standing competitor merged with another company in the suburbs, and the owner subsequently passed away. However, whenever I stop to reminisce about those days, I can still recall some good times. It got to the point where the owner and I would look at each other, trade some business small talk, and of course, smile with respect for each other.

Another thing happened in my small business that forced me to reach a higher level of proficiency. And I'll never forget this! The year was 1989, and we started getting requests from our customers about imprinted t-shirts. After saying, "No, we don't print t-shirts," many times, we decided to investigate the area of "silk-screen printing of t-shirts," which eventually became an excellent source of revenue and led to a completely new department in our business. This story, written by Jeffrey McCracken, was featured in *Crain's Detroit Business* as we celebrated our 10th anniversary in 1996. Today, we are a leading expert in the field, and continue to print t-shirts, sportswear, and advertising specialties for our customers.

As your proficiency level increases, you will develop a knack for adding specific departments to your own business structure that can improve your overall productivity. It is very important to concentrate on your best angle for production, promotion, and profits. Don't get so busy that when you're asked what your business is all about, you simply shrug your shoulders and say, "Good question, I'm still figuring that one out!" Remember to slow down.

Finally, learn to maximize your proficiency level. As you become more confident in your abilities, challenges will emerge. This might test your wherewithal, knowledge, or progress as a small business owner. Hang in there. Learn to meet these challenges with determination, answer the tough questions with dignity, and accept the differences that result from each new situation. With time, effort, energy, and a good nudge/push from your real supporters, your enhanced level of proficiency will be inevitable. You will get there, smile with confidence, and win.

Chapter 4

MARKET YOURSELF AND YOUR BUSINESS

ENOUGH CANNOT BE SAID about marketing. Once discovered, the importance of marketing goes far beyond the initial scope of maintaining and advancing your business. Simply defined, marketing is comprised of all the things you do today that may bring in the revenue tomorrow. It is sometimes the subtle ways, and oftentimes the overt actions that you perform to keep your company's name in the eyes of the general public. In many cases, the day that you are out marketing your business, your sales may be low for that particular day, however, improving your long-range sales plan is the ultimate goal.

For example, we greatly benefited from our Alexis Company Fun Run, which was initially launched in May of 1989 to support the Ms. Wheelchair Michigan Association. The event served both as a community event and fundraiser that created an exciting time for many of our regular customers, friends, business associates, neighbors, and family members to come together. The afternoon was quite enjoyable with refreshments, prizes, and healthy fun, while supporting a local nonprofit organization. Meanwhile, it helped to serve a good cause and enabled us to market our business.

The goodwill and publicity which are gained from promoting such an event carry a lot of weight in the community. This makes people aware of the "giving nature" associated with your business and provides insight into another avenue or dimension of your company. In essence, you become the hero by giving a little time and energy to support others. This is a great way to stay in business.

Of course, whenever we promote an event of this magnitude, all of the participants wear Alexis Company t-shirts—which by the way, is free publicity—and the word-of-mouth from person to person is so extensive that new business comes "knocking at your door." It can be quite an experience when you start to bring in new customers on a regular basis. In fact, the experience gained from sponsoring a community event will maximize your chances of surviving, thriving, and staying alive, exponentially.

As I reflect on these occasions, we have partnered with many local schools, churches, non-profit organizations, small businesses, associations, and local community groups—too many to name in this brief exercise.

Marketing requires creativity, imagination, brainstorming, and a good feeling of what may or may not work. I have personally enjoyed marketing my business at local school "Career Days." After a brief discussion about our business progress and success, many of the students are interested in part-time employment and summer jobs. Also, the teachers who are impressed with the presentation are equally excited about placing orders for their own professional and personal needs. In any economic climate, business comes and goes.

But, with a consistent marketing strategy, you can keep your business steady and readily available to take advantage of many opportunities that come your way.

To stay in business, a manager must know the difference between marketing, sales, advertising, and promoting. They are four distinct areas that can enhance your business output, depending on how you incorporate them into your system. Briefly, **advertising** is paying for a specific type of service associated with a specific time to promote your business. The many avenues include radio, newspapers, popular weekly magazines, internet promotions, and online email services.

The activity of generating **sales** is the dollar-for-dollar value of getting your products and services to your customers. This is done with maintaining a strategy to maximize your profits. When you decide to give away free ink pens or key rings with your company's name or emblem printed on them, you are **promoting** your business. And, as stated earlier, **marketing** is the extra stuff you do to bring your business into the limelight without adding pressure to either yourself or to your audience. It's the way that you stay in the public eye, which helps to keep customers' focus on receiving products, goods, and services from your business.

You can market your business many ways. Listed below are some great suggestions that we have used which led to significant results and increased sales. Your goal is to remain profitable, visible, and impactful. You can become really creative in orchestrating events and extra activities that bring more attention to your business. Here is our list of some of the wonderful activities that served as part of our marketing strategy, which were beneficial:

a) Fun Run Festival

b) Community Thank You Cook Out

c) Local School Concert Fundraiser

d) Customer Appreciation Gift Certificates

e) Birthday Recognition and Free Gift

f) Civic Organization Convention Booth

g) Participation in Festivals, Parades and Bazaars

h) Collaborating with Other Businesses

i) Radio Interviews for Business Owners

j) Open House Event with Refreshments

You get the idea. Expand on this list, because there are so many ways that you can gain a sense of on-going presence in the eyes of your customers.

To stay in business, you must learn how and when to use the different methods and approaches to advance your company. For example, advertising can be helpful, but it is extremely costly, especially if you select the wrong target market. What is the **target market**? That's the specific group of consumers you are focusing on, with the goal of selling your products to them. You want to captivate their attention and get them buying specifically from you. Very importantly, making sales does not mean much without foreseeable profit or growth. You must learn how to establish your own pricing system that works for your company.

Additionally, how you choose to promote your small business is essential for gaining customers from various markets. And, when you market your business, you should already have an idea of what your expectations are, based upon your input, depth, and performance level. Marketing yourself and your business is an on-going process, and it's mandatory to stay in business over time.

PHOTO GALLERY – SECTION 1

I was named after my first cousin, **Alexis Jane Johnson Hill**, because my mother wanted me to "Be smart like Jane," and go to college. I did and graduated.

Just the two of us together, now me and my daughter **Sequina**, who was six years old when we opened the store on Gratiot Avenue.

My brother **Ronnie** attended many children's birthday parties;
he was probably the first **Black clown** in their homes.

The **"Light Up Rose"** is our first novelty product and remains my favorite. We
sold hundreds of them during the **Prince Purple Rain Tour from 1984 to 1985**.

My nephew Samuel III and my brother Ronnie have been
my right and left hand throughout this journey.

Our customers support the business and love our merchandise,
service, approach, and commitment to excellence.

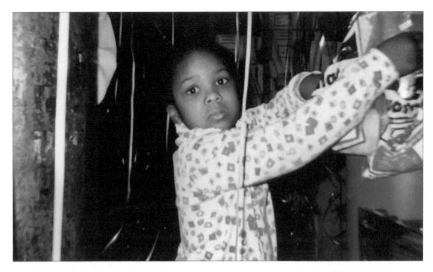

My niece **Santrice** was only six years old when she blew up balloons for Mayor Dennis Archer's Inauguration in 1993. Years later, when she was 19, she sold novelties at the Mardi Gras parades in New Orleans, Louisiana in 2009. (below)

Rhapsody, Louis, and Samuel are seated while Shareen and Tony
(near the truck) prepare for our "Rain or Shine, It's Festival Time"
in Highland, Park, Michigan.

The legendary **Vandellas** of Motown Records visit my radio show, "Let's Talk
About It," in **1997 at WHPR 88.1 FM** in Highland Park, Michigan.
Thank you, Mr. R. J. Watkins, Manager.

My mother and I enjoyed the Hart Plaza Festivals downtown Detroit.
Here we are in 2002 with Detroit City Councilwoman Maryann Mahaffey
(deceased 2006); she always supported our small business.

My sister-in-law **Janice** gets ready for a busy day of customer service on **Valentine's Day in 1990.**

Wally Well Apple from the Wellness Plan joins us in 1995
for our festival in Highland Park, Michigan.

Mr. E. Donald Sherman, my photographer and professional consultant
for more than 20 years, captured the history, progress, success stories,
and various programs that were sponsored by The Alexis Company.

When we reached our 10th Anniversary, I was elated and we celebrated in a big way with a party at our store. My mother and I, along with my dear friend **Joyce Keener**, were delighted about the steady progress and future potential.

For our **10th Anniversary**, everyone played their part. **Sequina and Kimberly** blew up the balloons, and we had a live performance from the **Gratitude Steel Band**. The community and special guests were invited to come and share with us on that wonderful day.

Margo DeRamus, my Spiritual Mother, gave inspiring words of encouragement, direction, and leadership.

Mr. Paul Taylor, Director of Inner City Sub Center, brought several young men to expose them to entrepreneurship and the journey of a small business owner.

The guests included family, friends, neighbors, church members, customers, small business owners, as well as civic and community leaders. **Mr. Chester Vaughn** of **Blackness Unlimited** gave his remarks.

My first boss, **Mr. James R. Thompson, CPA, tax attorney**, was proud to attend the 10th Anniversary of my small business, The Alexis Company. I was 15 years old when hired as a clerk-typist at **Thompson & Edwards, CPAs in 1972.**

Choir members from Unity Baptist Church supported our
10th Anniversary; Denise Griffin and Ronnie are seated with me.
Another friend, Denise, is standing with Patty Mitchell.

My mother sang her favorite solo, "Precious Lord,"
at the celebration. Sing, Mama!

Above: My neighbors, **Ronald and Mikal Connell**, who lived above our store, were there with me and Sam to congratulate us.
Below: Councilman Earl and Mrs. Naomi Wheeler of Highland Park, Michigan were avid supporters of The Alexis Company.

By 1993, we had become a viable small business in the City of Detroit, and gave a fundraiser to support the campaign to elect Dennis Archer for Mayor.

The candidate for Mayor listened to my concerns as a small business owner.

Dr. Tomell DuBose and **Attorney Reney DuBose** are standing with Archer campaign team member **Victoria Inniss** and myself at the event.

Left: Rhapsody, Sharon, and Patty were quite helpful during the fundraiser.
Right: My daughter and I were so happy. Below: My cousin Mary is standing
with **Sheila Hale, owner of Everett's Cornrows**, and **Victoria Innis**.

Enthusiastic campaign staff rally and support the candidate for Mayor.

Chapter 5

YOUR HEALTH, YOUR STRENGTH, AND YOUR RIGHT MIND

YOUR PHYSICAL MOMENTUM IS highly dependent on maintaining a healthy lifestyle that is compatible with the demands of small business ownership. A healthy outlook—despite economic conditions—for your business can weather any storm. The better you take care of yourself, often results in a positive future for your company. Your health, your strength, and your right mind are the key assets to capitalize upon. Your brain is the seat of intellectual power, and you must learn how to use it effectively to accomplish your business goals.

Sadly enough, it is very easy to fall into a pattern of bad habits that can drastically affect your physical health. Many small business owners and managers are "high energy" people, so the propensity to slow down, relax, and eat a well-balanced diet is sometimes a hard pill to swallow. It can become difficult to master if you are running around on empty—with poor nutrition—day after day. Slow starters who are in business, often need a boost of energy to get moving. This can also lead to very bad habits that send erratic messages to your brain, physical makeup, and biological system.

At any rate, to stay in business, you need to develop good habits and evaluate your actions to maintain good overall health. Your physical health, body strength, and mental capacity are the key components to examine, which will improve your output, given the high demands that occur in small business. I believe that many small business owners and managers suffer from not getting regular checkups, being extremely emotional, lacking adequate rest, suffering from information overload, having very poor eating habits, succumbing to high stress levels, and indulging short tempers.

As quiet as it's kept, these are just some of the areas which can cause sickness and distress. They can lead to serious bodily ailments, deficiencies, and the abuse of substances for quick remedies. If possible, minimize your level of stressful situations. Many physical problems are the direct result of unresolved conflict and intense circumstances gone way out of control. In my own career as a counselor, I learned the importance of managing your emotions.

Several years ago, in 2014, I traveled to a convention in St. Louis, Missouri, along with members from my church at that time. The conference focused on ways to improve Christian education at your local church. The event included an area designated to health care vendors who were providing a whole gamut of information about many different illnesses. Although I have been blessed to monitor and maintain good health most of my life, I picked up the literature and saved it for the bus trip home.

As I read the information about stroke, heart disease, diabetes, various cancers, high blood pressure, colds, influenza, and so much more, I noticed one common element listed on every brochure: "Get plenty of rest." This guidance appeared in the sections on how to prevent these illnesses from occurring in one's life. This really stuck in my mind, because they resonated with what my own mother often said:

"You don't get enough rest." When I was a child, my mother would interrupt my playtime with my friends and order: "Get off the porch! I need to get my rest!"

Today, especially when your business is growing in leaps and bounds, you need to get a good night's rest. It makes all the difference in the world of decision-making, interacting with others, and maximizing your opportunities in small business.

So, it's very important to be in tune with your own emotional and physical state of mind. Knowing your capacity for tolerance and the "hot buttons" of your personality can prevent unnecessary illnesses that decrease your productivity. Be true to yourself, true to your customers, true to your staff, and true to your loved ones. If you're having a "bad day," admit it, and make a good attempt to avoid conflict for that particular day.

Learn how to take care of yourself by engaging in some type of relaxation regimen that will help you take it easy. Calm your spirit. Give your mind and body a well-deserved break. Get some rest. Take a weekend vacation. You can go for a long drive while listening to your favorite music or motivational speaker. Refresh yourself as you take time to prepare for the next business prospect. And, take time to breathe!

Remember, another great business deal or opportunity is just around the corner. And the question that you have to answer is, will you be ready to take advantage of the situation and capitalize upon it? If you're worn out, worn down, or downright tired—physically, mentally, and emotionally—you won't be at your best behavior to conduct business and execute that particular deal!

Finally, it's helpful if you make a list of your own bad habits that are detrimental to maintaining good health. Now this task takes some real, honest introspection. We're often very good at recognizing our strengths, but not equally as sure about our weaknesses. You might suffer from excessive smoking, over-consumption of alcohol, the use of drugs (prescribed or recreational), the lack of regular exercise, improper diet, too many sweets, and of course, being a fast-food fanatic. Stop procrastinating and move forward by correcting and changing the abusive patterns that prevent you from having a healthy, prosperous lifestyle. All of these factors can impact your ability to stay in business. Remember, the better your health, your strength, and your mental state, the more you can achieve in your small business. Prosperity is a direct result of maintaining a clean, healthy, productive, and worthwhile lifestyle.

On a personal note, I can remember when I was a professional guidance counselor and psychologist in the community mental health field from 1978 until 1991. I had direct contact with people who suffered from depression, loneliness, anger management, personality disorders, passive-aggressive tendencies, substance abuse issues, hallucinations, delusions, and side effects from psychotropic medications used in treatment for their emotional pain.

Some of my clients were quite disheveled, overweight, skinny, and physically out of sorts, and they lacked a good support system. They depended upon special programs that the federal government implemented for their population. A full team of professionals were involved with the quality of care. This included the social worker, counselor, psychiatrist, nurse, primary care physician, occupational therapist, and physical therapist. The primary goal was to help them maintain their emotional stability by providing coping mechanisms and helping them reconnect to society.

So, that's why I started a small business that focused on helping others share their love and making people smile, by providing ways to simply have FUN. Hence, our slogan, "Where the FUN Begins..." I had heard enough sad stories. I needed to cheer myself up as well, because in 1986, I was going through my own divorce from my high school sweetheart, which was quite a painful experience. True love really hurts!

It was time to remove myself from handling the mental and emotional problems of others in a professional setting. I wanted a change and a different focus for my life. I yearned for a better outlook on life, despite the shattered dreams of my marriage. I needed a new environment that could bring me some joy, some money, and some peace in order to move past this drama and raise our daughter. My health, my strength, and my right mind depended on it. This small business became the outcome because it was my new focus.

The opportunity to start my small business came at the right time when I needed it most. It was a pleasant escape. No, frankly speaking, I did not have a business plan. I did not have any financial backing or influential business friends. No, I did not have a lot of information about the business that I wound up developing. No, I did not have a mentor at that time. But I had faith. That's all I had was faith.

I had the belief that life was meant to be enjoyed, and when bad things happen, they eventually will pass on by. I had: a strong family system; great parents who shared their love, time, and energy; and close friends who understood me, listened to my concerns, and let me cry. I had my deliberate faith in God, and my brothers, who taught me to compete in order to exist in *their* world.

I had some great teachers throughout my journey, on all my levels of schooling. My precious daughter is a special blessing who motivated me to continue striving for excellence. And I was blessed with a deep desire to continue to live and do well, in spite of the discomfort, disappointment, and defeat!

And so, The Alexis Company, also known as Alexis Novelty & Gifts, was born.

Chapter 6

Minimize Your Notes Payable

"Nobody owns me!"

I declared that to my supervisor in 1983. I was bold, brass, and unafraid. And at the time, I didn't own a business. I just wanted to make it clear that I was my own person. Mind you, we returned to Detroit from living in New York City where we had no family or close associations. We were the first college graduates in our families. Actually, my husband had finished law school while I worked as a supervisor at a Jewish agency in their community program in midtown Manhattan. Our daughter, who was born on the first day of law school, was the icing on the cake!

We learned how to make it on our own and did quite well, given the circumstances. Somehow those words came out of my mouth while I was having a one-on-one conversation with her about "moving up in one's career." Learning how to control your mind, time, and direction has always been my goal. I never liked subtle favoritism in any form. My parents worked hard and taught us to value employment. They told us to use your brain and your talents to move up any ladder. My mother's favorite phrase was, "Take what you have and make what you can out of it." For me and my brothers, this was our family mandate.

As a small business owner, it's easy to fall into the trap of debt that you may acquire while pursuing your dream. On the one hand, your concentration is so focused on building your empire, while the other hand is trying to manage the staggering amount of notes payable that seem to be accumulating at an alarming rate! If you're not careful and do not choose a well-planned financial strategy, you may incur more and more debt without clear direction.

This can especially become a problem if you have good credit, because it makes you a prime target for lending agencies that offer you long-term loans. If you're not careful, you may never get above water to swim. I know that uncanny feeling when you make a substantial profit, only to realize that it's the exact amount necessary to pay a major bill. Yes, instead of having more capital to operate your business, the significant funds end up paying a "balance due."

Another thing that I learned to stay in business, is that you must be wise and sensible enough to evaluate your overall needs for additional capital to operate. What are the parameters to obtain the necessary funding to develop and expand your business? Think it over before committing to more debt.

Without proper management and guidance, it's easy to become a target for frequent loans, home equity financing, and excessive credit card debt. You don't want to become overwhelmed by having too many monthly payments that consume your sales projections and profit margins. Robert Kiyosaki, author of *Rich Dad, Poor Dad,* calls it symptoms of the "rat race.[2]" It also reminds me of that famous verse in the Holy Bible in Proverbs 22:7 (KJV): "The rich rule over the poor, and the borrower is slave to the lender."

If you wind up with too many monthly notes to pay, this can tap into your mindset and debilitate your creative thinking skills. Instead of working on the next big idea for your company, you'll be worrying about how to pay that extra note! Cash flow is imperative to succeed in sales, profits, and long-term business forecasting. So, stay on top of how your notes are paid and how many you have. Question the need for more and more notes payable as your business grows and matures. You do not want your sales to come in one door, and immediately go out another door, right into the hands of the bill collectors. And most bill collectors expect to be paid on time, every time.

By the time I figured out what it meant to have "business savvy" or understand terms like "business acumen," I was $40,000 in debt, and that did not include my student loans from attending college! I did not know the difference between "good debt" and "bad debt" until 2003. At that time, I'd been functioning in business undauntedly for 17 years.

Learning to manage and harness your cash flow can be extremely challenging, but it's a worthwhile task in the long run to keep you from having large sums of bad debt. Excessive debt can kill a good business, no matter how hard you work. To avoid having trouble with creditors and bill collecting agencies, ask yourself some questions: What's the purpose of this new debt? Is it for new equipment, supplies, or research and development of a new product line? Do we need it to upgrade our office or to expand our marketing goals? Will the debt create additional opportunities? Is it a necessity? For example, will it help to increase our profits? Are the time frames reasonable for repayment and in accordance with our goals? Perhaps this is a move to add funds that will be used for training and staff development. Review your questions and purposes for acquiring more debt. And proceed with caution, looking both ways.

Because no matter how much the additional funds may benefit your business and are used, at some point you will want to get rid of the debt. If you focus and are determined to keep your business free and clear from an abundance of debt, and move more into the arena of the abundance of wealth, you will stay in business a very long time. You will avoid the hassle of being financially overwhelmed with constantly paying out money. A good business entity operates properly, and will keep a smile on your face.

Chapter 7

BAD CUSTOMERS, SITUATIONS & CIRCUMSTANCES

A GOOD CUSTOMER IS the best customer for a small business. Most business owners want to have good customers 100% of the time. However, every now and then, you should expect to encounter a bad customer, and the catch is: will you be ready? Or better yet, how will you be ready to handle the situation or circumstances that may surround the event?

Others will say that the customer is always right. But in actuality, some customers are misinformed or uncertain. Sometimes they're having their own "bad day." Others just have a mean-spirited agenda. As a business owner, you must know how to respond and handle those individual cases before things really get out of control. You may need to address an issue where something did not go smoothly with a customer's order. Sometimes you have to stop and listen to your heart for guidance on how do just that when handling customer situations.

Whenever I stop and evaluate a customer's complaint, concern, or potential problem, I wisely take into consideration their facial expression, tone of voice, and choice of words (drawing from my counseling skills). The dialogue to resolve the conflict is extremely important once all of the circumstantial evidence has been presented and examined. My goal, in this case, is to maintain a sense of control and stability while focusing on finding a tangible solution that, once again, leads to another *satisfied* customer. I want to resolve the issue in a very positive vein to promote a continued customer relationship that is healthy and moves forward.

This is not always an easy task, because some instances may demand your immediate attention, just as a new patron is entering your business location or environment to purchase an item. To stay in business despite these uncomfortable situations, you must be able to think on your feet and respond quickly with authority and demonstrate good leadership. Handle each problem with dignity and respect to all of the parties involved.

The basic survival of a small business is maintaining good customer relations and managing those extraneous situations that may provoke conflict. Good leadership skills are a necessity to stay in a small business. Learn them, practice them, and use them appropriately. Always be ready to do your best to resolve conflict within and throughout your business environment.

Here's a true story. Approximately one year after we started printing t-shirts for the general public, I learned that even though you may do everything correctly 99% of the time, things can still go south. I was excited that we had a new client who ordered t-shirts for an event. Even though she had signed our company's written agreement with the exact specifications and quantity, there was an obvious discrepancy when she picked them up two weeks later. Despite my efforts to resolve the problem and make the correction, she was not satisfied. Instead, she filed a case in small claims court. I totally disagreed with the decision, but the outcome fell upon my shoulders and we had to pay $350, plus the court fees to settle the case! With those types of customers, the task at hand, as well as the financial loss, you never forget. I can still remember her full name, to this day! However, the learning experience was worth the trouble.

Yet all in all, it's been more than 35 years now of small business success, and I can truly say that we have had fewer than 10—maybe eight at the most—"bad customers" out of the thousands of customers that we have served. And in each case where there was some concern, we properly addressed the issue, solved the problem, and regained the customer's respect. Customers Are Really Everything. Take care of your customers, and they will take care of you and your business for many years to come. That's why we CARE.

Chapter 8

DEVELOP ADJUNCT PARTNERS

IN MY OPINION, SOME of the best partners for a small business are the professional people whom you can count on to support you, and who are not directly on your weekly payroll. These are people who can refer others to your store for products and services. They are the special persons in your business circle who admire what you are doing as a small business owner. They highly respect your ambition and goals. These are the ones, the generous people who will go out of their way to tell their own boss about your business, which in turn, can bring you more business. These individuals relieve your worry about self-promoting, because they are doing that for you! It's wonderful, and boosts your ego. They help you believe in you, and that is phenomenal. It is amazing!

Adjunct partners are usually gifted and talented people in their own right. Their personal skills can enhance any aspect or layer of your business objectives. Many of my partners are good with computer graphics, public relations, law, accounting, marketing, business techniques, financial planning, and social work. They come from various professions and walks of life. They are the people who believe in you and give your small business the strength to keep on serving your customers. When they place their "stamp of approval" upon your shoulders, you're bound for greatness.

That's what happened to us when I met a wonderful lady in 1989 who assisted with our first Fun Run Festival. She shared her knowledge and helped us get professional letterhead, envelopes, and additional stationery with our business logo printed on the stock. Then we sent letters to invite others to attend and support the venture. Her expertise in leadership was vast and extensive, given her work history in state government and experience with handling mainstream supervisors. She embraced the business, which led to our company printing t-shirts for her own travel group. They went to the Super Bowl every year and became one of our long-standing customers for 25 years. Their big order for 2020 came in February, just before the shutdown of the US economy in March due to COVID-19. Ahead of the official pandemic!

The adjunct partners who care about what you're doing are often people who can provide specific services to help your business grow. Believe me, they can provide services that will save you thousands of dollars that you might pay by hiring someone else. They are usually experts in their fields.

They're eager to assist you when necessary, and because of their own career status, they can offer you the best options. They also have the ability to make your business stand out from the competition. They are excellent advisors and sometimes, just a good "sounding board." Many of the partners whom we have acquired over the years have grown to become our special friends. They are people who give honest feedback and make significant suggestions that can help to improve our overall output. I highly respect their opinions and value their contribution. Really, they represent the cheerleading team for your small business. It makes the work tolerable and fun.

For instance, I had an adjunct partner, who by the way was a dentist, who told me during a dry spell about the importance of reaching out to new customers. She encouraged us to expand our networking to obtain new business and search for new markets that could benefit from our products and services. This is important, because you want to avoid contacting the same customers to support your business, to prevent being redundant. Keep them connected and smiling. And take the time to stretch out and reach for new markets by reviewing that stack of business cards you've collected from all those special parties and networking events. It can be worthwhile and possibly generate a completely new list of patrons.

I got the idea of keeping a fishbowl on a stand at the entrance of my store from an adjunct partner. This served to encourage our patrons to drop in their business cards for future drawings, prizes, and birthday celebrations. It also created a "constant contact list" and opportunity for new business. This "fishbowl" technique was well before the email service now called "Constant Contact." The relationships forged through adjunct partners build a unique method of stability, as people interact and grow personally by attaching themselves to the life of an entrepreneur.

Chapter 9

KEY PEOPLE
MAKE THE DIFFERENCE

IN EVERY ORGANIZATION, BUSINESS entity, school setting, church, and family system, key people make things run smoothly. In fact, without these individuals, the entire operation would simply fall apart. They are essential and make up a significant piece of the puzzle. They are the main people of the system. These special individuals are the glue that holds all of the remaining pieces together. Without their input and support, things would go awry. They are the ones who hold the major positions to guarantee the continued progress and steady hand of an already existing system.

You may have heard the terms "the buck stops here," and "I call the shots," or "I'm the main man!" In other words, what they're really saying is that, "I am the decision-maker for this group. Nothing gets done without my approval or input!"

The title can vary from mother, to secretary, to security personnel, to administrative assistant, to bookkeeper, to vice president, and so on. But the most important thing of all, is that they are the gatekeepers and have the keys to let you in or to keep you out of the mainstream of that particular organization. While the President of the United States of America has Secret Service Agents, key people play an essential role in helping to protect the chairperson or most important leader of any establishment.

They can make it easy or difficult for you to meet the book-keeper who actually signs the checks, or the project manager who just might be waiting on your proposal for 10,000 whistles. They may know the whereabouts of the coordinator of that special event who is planning to launch a big marketing promotion. Great business opportunities are often fortified because of the key person who politely says, "One moment please, I'll let them know you're here. They're in the boardroom waiting for you to present your proposal." Wow! That's it! Here comes the chance of a lifetime for your business. Do it!

As a small business owner, you want to be well-received in each case. Your behavior when you meet the key person is sometimes a matter of life or the death of another business opportunity. In many situations, you don't know how far or how deep this chance will go. So, put your best approach forward. It's to your benefit, especially in the long run. Let this opportunity run wide and deep.

For example, we had no idea that when the choir director of a local high school was made aware of our store, it would lead to other department heads and teachers in that particular school placing orders for our products and services. The revenue generated from them was approximately $10,000 in one year through the interaction, coordination, and internal mechanism of the school.

Word-of-Mouth is the most powerful form of advertising. My daughter (who was a member of the choir) simply stated, "My mommy prints t-shirts." I was ecstatic and overwhelmed at the same time! It's been 25 years now, and we are still printing t-shirts for the choral program at that local high school. I love them, appreciate them, and enjoy their concerts and performances.

Yes, key people play a very important role, which can lead to huge profits or major distress! As a small business owner, I believe it is in your best interest to recognize their authority, faithfulness, and attitude—while aiming to gain their respect. They are very important to the organization. They are serious-minded and protect the interest of the boss, supervisor, or manager who is in charge of the overall budget and decision-making process for new accounts.

Your task, if you decide to take this assignment, is to find out who, in fact, handles the major issues that have the greatest impact within the organization. Make a strong effort to develop a connection and a working relationship with them that will benefit the objectives of your business goals.

Finally, I encourage you to **respect** key people, get to know them, and maintain a positive relationship with them. They are human beings who work extremely hard and have real feelings, too. Treat them well. And please don't take them for granted. This will help you stay in business much longer, for sure.

Photo Gallery – Section 2

The **Million Man March in 1995** was a phenomenal event in Washington, DC. My daughter and I were amongst the few women present to witness this historical event!

Sequina and I sold t-shirts, caps, and Black History posters throughout the 15-hour day. As the crowds gathered, local reporters captured this moment where men pledged to change their lives. They came in droves by bus, car, train—by any means, to get there.

By the 20th year of business, our Detroit Souvenirs were sold at the **Cobo Convention Center** in downtown Detroit.

Our 20th Anniversary celebration was held at the fabulous **Roostertail** in Detroit, Michigan. Every guest signed their name on my giant t-shirt board. Simply marvelous!

Above: My partner and graphics designer **Arthur Williams** and his wife Shanell enjoyed the celebration. **Below: Jaunice Flowers** presented a beautiful poem written especially for me.

My cousins, **Jewel Jones and Mary Grant**, as well as **Mrs. Rosie Colman** (Lewis and Kimberly's mom), had a good time.

Here are some church members who supported the business over the years: Jackie, Yvonne, Juanita, Rose, and Angela are standing with me.

Trina creates a lot of attention while selling merchandise in front of the store.

This little girl loved tooting her trumpet throughout the day at the Highland Park Festival. My nephew **Steven** led our **Kiddie Klown Patrol**. He's a star!

Face painting is a hit at our events, and my cousin **Janice Robinson** teaches the youth to follow her lead.

The **Ruff Ryders Motorcycle Club** discussed safety with the youth at our local **Neighborhood Festival in 2008.**

In **2005**, *Attorney Sharon McPhail* supported local small businesses at our **Families Are Forever Conference** held at the St. Regis Hotel in Detroit.

My cousin **Rufus** shares his truck driving skills with the students attending our Neighborhood Festival in 2008.

My brother **William Dwayne and his son Steven** managed
our booth at the **Michigan State Fair in 2006**.

The Alexis Company staff members take a bow for a job well done after a long,
busy, and exciting day at our local **Neighborhood Festival in 2008**.

My family showed up for the **Midwest Civic Council of Block Clubs' Garage Sale. The Alexis Company, Metro Foods Center, and local businesses** supported the event in 2014. Here's **Steven, Sequina, Samuel, Dwayne, and myself.**

We have learned so much about the local and small business community by participating in the **Midwest Civic Council of Block Clubs**. Members were present and enthusiastic for neighborhood development and growth in 2014.

Our 25th Anniversary was **"An Evening in Opera and Song," presenting Sequina DuBose and friends: Fredrick Jackson, Rebecca Comerford, David Hughey, Issachah Savage, and Tedrin Blair Lindsay.** The event was held at Orchestra Hall in Detroit in June 2011. These artists are now accomplished experts in their respective fields of classical music and business.

My family: **Mr. & Mrs. Ronald and Janice Hinkle, Sr.; Miss Santrice Hinkle; and Mr. & Mrs. William and Marsha Hinkle** enjoyed the wonderful evening.

Our special guests savored the atmosphere of the VIP reception
before the musical performance, which was magnificent!

My mentors from **Thompson & Edwards, CPAs (1972): Russell Halleen;**
another couple; **Sequina; Janet Halleen; and Rick and Ann Edwards**
take part in the celebration of our 25th Anniversary. It was amazing!

Mrs. Ivory Underwood with her daughters and **Mrs. Shirley Johnson** spend a moment with **Sequina** before the concert.

As an entrepreneur who loves to dream, I got the opportunity to pursue a brief career as a gospel recording artist. Here, I'm singing with **Robert Anderson and the group in 2001** (our 15th Anniversary) at Wayne State University Community Arts Auditorium.

Also in 1991, I participated and sang at **Young Artists for Christ Workshop** (presented by Michael Brooks) where **I met gospel recording superstar Yolanda Adams!**

Over the years as I've been a small business owner, my family has been the faithful, stabilizing force that kept the magic going. **Below:** Here is **Rudolph Emange (Cameroon). Next Page Top: Ronnie, Rufus, Dwayne, and Steven** holding the guitar. **Next Page Bottom:** The ladies hanging with **Mom, Marsha, Dr. Shelley, Marsha No. 2, Jackie, and Vernice.** Celebrate life and be peaceful. *Regina* - **2021**

Special thanks to my Chairpersons who supported and directed the vision of my 35th Anniversary Celebration and Book Release. You are appreciated for your amazing talent, insight, knowledge, consideration, and organizational skills. I am truly blessed and grateful to God that you are my team. I love you all.

**Dr. DaNita
Weddle
Chairperson**

**Mr. Arthur Williams, Program Chairperson, and
Ms. Sheri Burton, Marketing/Sales Chairperson.**

Chapter 10

TRAIN, TRAIN, TRAIN

TRAINING IS THE PROCESS by which we learn a task, responsibility, skill, or talent. Training is the most important aspect of any successful, small business. It includes the methods by which you teach others how to do the business in an effective way that leads to high profits and many satisfied customers. A satisfied customer is one who returns to your business on several occasions. Over time, your training regimen will indicate how well your team functions, and give you a clear measure of your level of success. You must train your staff, customers, suppliers, supporters, and yourself. But before we get into the details about how to do that, we'll discuss what is training. Let's talk about how we train others, and why training is the primary ingredient for longevity in small business.

By definition, to train means to tutor, teach, enlighten, educate, inform, instruct, or guide someone, according to Webster's New World Dictionary.[3] It also means to make skillful or proficient, to point in an exact position, or to undergo a course of instruction or preparation. Training involves systematic instruction that leads to the development of specific habits, thoughts, or behaviors that support an individual to become skillful in some work or task by teaching or practicing. It is done regularly and constantly. The process involves the necessary activity to teach others how to do their duties, learn the responsibilities, and develop their attitude that is associated with their own personal disposition. Over a significant period, the training is complete and put into action, and the goal is accomplished. Many opportunities provide continued growth and development, once the initial structure has been achieved.

It takes creativity, ingenuity, energy, and desire to train people. Of course, many models are available to promote your business goals and desire for excellence. However, most individuals have not experienced the power of a well-trained skill or talent until they apply at your operation. Unfortunately, in today's society, the idea of work ethic, continuity, spring-board success, and a guided pathway to personal achievement and fulfillment in the workforce is rapidly dying. As society changes, needs change, people change, and the value of maintaining "good work habits" has definitely changed. The huge distraction of the day has infiltrated the work environment, as employees are consumed with the information that "pops up" on their cell phones and various mobile devices.

However, as a small business manager seeking to stay in business for the long haul, you must develop your own tactics for training your staff members. How to train other people is an art in itself. It takes patience and consistency. Your team must be informed about the goals and the future direction of the business. They must be aware of your concerns as the growth of your business begins to take shape and forms into the "the next big thing." They should respect your code of ethics and policies in order to function effectively throughout the establishment. They must know the requirements for the job and be willing to perform their duties. They need to be flexible to the demands of the moment, and their response to customer service.

As a leader, you should be honest, direct, and succinct when training others. They should know your expectations in all aspects, and be able to execute them according to the Policy and Procedures Manual of your business. The written information can serve as a guide for everyone who is involved in sales, marketing, promotions, and management of the company.

Train people by using the power of humor with good examples, and sharing honestly, when you have dealt with some difficult situations. Capture their attention by giving good explanations that resonate with them. Be able to relate and meet them on their level. When you train people, you are giving them the power that they need in order to function adequately in their position, job, or role at your place of business. Everyone should grow in their abilities, leading to higher productivity, and greater expectations for the future of your small business. That's when **they all** believe in your dream!

Without training, your small business will become a disaster. Training is the element that will push a small business to thrive year after year, and remain successful in the community. As time goes by, new methods emerge, customer requests become demanding, product lines change, and different trends begin to influence the economy. It becomes more important to make the adjustments and train your staff members. You will want everyone in your operation to be well trained, because they represent you.

Members of your establishment must know what pleases you as a manager, owner, or president of a small business. They must know how important it is that every customer is treated with dignity and respect. They should dress appropriately, according to your company's dress code or uniform standards. They should exhibit good personal habits, a healthy attitude, and have adequate verbal skills, even when the day is challenging. Training ensures that your business operates proficiently, even in your absence due to a meeting, conference, personal illness, or vacation.

By June of 1998, a dozen years into The Alexis Company, I knew that I had done a great job in training, because I was able to take a three-week trip to Ghana, West Africa, with a local high school choir. My nephew, who was 24 years old at that time, had been working with me since he was 14, and did an excellent job running our store. I was very impressed, given the reports from my customers and his outstanding leadership and management skills.

Why is training so important? How can it be the bread and butter that helps sustain your small business? Because it reduces chaos, confusion, conflict, and concerns. Denounce things that may attempt to invade your territory or progress. Training provides the mechanism to select staff, place them in specific positions such as cashier, receptionist, printer, stock clerk, assistant manager, etcetera. Teach them their roles and watch the results with confidence. Your business will run smoothly and efficiently, with fewer interruptions or disappointments. Avoid getting side-tracked. Stick with a proven format.

Once we identified the clientele of our small business, we created a strategy to train everyone who was associated with The Alexis Company. As we evaluated the many people who were involved with the business, we noticed four groups who were the main characters that impacted our success. They were our staff members, our customer base, the suppliers who provided our product line, and our personal supporters. As the owner and manager of the company, I took the time to stop one day and said, "I need to train myself in some areas, too!"

Briefly speaking, your **staff members** are the "face" of the company and interact with your customers daily. They must know their responsibilities and duties in the position that you have hired them. They should also know in general, the who, what, when, where, and why about your business. This enables them to answer questions with confidence. They should be respectful and courteous.

I prefer people who know how to smile with a dose of enthusiasm. Depending upon the nature of your business, you need staff members who can be flexible and productive, especially during peak seasons. Their ability to adapt to the situation, culture, different trends, and economic changes is imperative for steady growth and development.

On some of our worst days, our business slogan—"Where the FUN Begins…"—helped to shift the atmosphere and remind us of our purpose. It's so important to foster a positive work environment that welcomes each customer and gets the job done effectively. Over time, your staff will gain a sense of responsibility, pride in their duties, flagrant eagerness, and reward for connecting emotionally with your establishment. They eventually will begin to function like they "own" the operation. We often rewarded excellent behavior with gifts, bonuses, merchandise, and genuine acts of kindness that were meaningful to each staff member.

My favorite employees have been young people between the ages of 13 and 25. I simply enjoy working with that age group that includes high school teens, college students, and young adults.

In fact, I have a "special clause" within their assigned duties. Beyond the regular chores associated with each job, I have three core, basic requirements that all students must follow in order to keep their job at The Alexis Company. Number one, they must **keep their personal room at home Clean.** Two, they must **complete their homework and get Good Grades.** And number three, they must **Follow Directions** at all times. We worked at many special events outside the actual store, such as festivals, parades, and bazaars. In large crowds, I needed them to pay attention to the environment. We built our establishment with a unique, business training program that benefited more than 92 youth and college students throughout our company's history.

Many of our **Customers** became friends after a few successful orders and contacts. When you make them feel comfortable and relaxed as you do business, you create an opportunity to enjoy small talk and to share their life problems or concerns. Sharing commonalities can be an excellent tool to build rapport and a style that leaves them feeling completely satisfied with every encounter at your business location.

Be aware of the opportunity for supporting special needs and requests, given their age and possible physical limitations. Your customers will love your concern and care for them and your desire to get things done decently, well within their budget. Bad habits, once recognized, should be identified gingerly and handled efficiently so as not to lose contact with a customer. For example, a customer may request a delivery to their home, but no one is there to accept the order, and then you receive a call late in the evening from someone asking, "Where's my order?" Your ability to handle each situation with clarity and respect in a timely fashion will keep them coming back with repeat orders over and over again.

But you must also train them. They should know your hours of operation, if you're available for special appointments, and if you're willing to attend a meeting with a committee at their office or in someone's home. Your customers will learn to depend on you for their specific needs in a consistent manner that helps to sustain your small business for many years.

Next, we have our **Suppliers.** I learned a long time ago to have accounts with many suppliers all over the country. After three years in business, we finally started to take in t-shirt orders. There was one major distributor in Michigan with whom we opened an account. As the summer progressed and the orders started pouring in, the distributor was running short on demand for certain colors, styles, and larger sizes, making it difficult for us to meet our customers' deadlines. I decided to reach out to other suppliers and distributors in different states to avoid losing customers due to these shortages during the hot, busy, summer season. This led to having more than 125 accounts with various suppliers nationwide.

Interestingly, over time the suppliers began to notice our ordering style, timing of the order, quantity, and need for meeting the deadlines, which is associated with the t-shirt industry. We made our presence known and began to receive direct inquiries from companies who wanted our business and money.

By 2002, we were acknowledged as a small business who garnered the need for Case Pricing status with our suppliers. We had consistently reached the annual volume requirement necessary for several years, so they gave us lower prices for our product line. This, of course, led to better communication, industry friendships, additional purchasing power, and a unique position amongst the suppliers. We, in turn, were able to offer better pricing and super deals to our customers with this new business status. Smart suppliers recognize good business owners and extend themselves to build great relationships. Our success was compatible, and ultimately led to the satisfaction of our customers.

As a visionary leader and businessperson, I often enjoyed festivals and events that were promoted by our company. We eventually began to sponsor walkathons, family reunion seminars, musicals, and family fun days. We also supported nonprofit organizations and participated in special events throughout the metropolitan region.

As we traveled this journey of building new relationships and entering different markets, we gained a following of Alexis Company **Supporters.** This was unplanned, but so fantastic! Our Supporters include family members, friends, neighbors, church associates, local entrepreneurs, city officials, radio announcers, singers, and many artists who have stood by our side. Many of them have natural skills or have been trained in areas that are necessary to make events turn out successful.

And they take the responsibility for making sure that refreshments are available. They provide a set-up and break-down crew, and they analyze the agenda and program for the day. Their focus is to do everything necessary to make sure that the event goes over well for all who attend and participate. We thrive on excellence and excellence is what we do.

The funny thing is that they never ask for any compensation. Instead, they tell us, "Thank you for letting us help and be a part of your vision." We love our **Supporters.** And they **love** us, too! As I reflect over the years, I was a young, Black female, and a divorcée, who was raising our daughter. I refused to give up on my goals and dreams, in spite of the circumstances that were confronting me and trying to claim my existence.

That fortitude, vision, stamina, drive, resilience, and enthusiasm for life, I believe, was contagious. Our supporters caught onto the wave and continued to drive the success of the business. This was bolstered by the fact that the training within any organization is the additional glue that will keep everyone and everything together on your road to progress, success, and longevity.

Finally, you must train **Yourself!** As a manager, owner, or president of a small business, it is so easy to forget about oneself. The status of an active entrepreneur creates a tremendous amount of responsibility, expectations, work assignments, and pressure. Before long, it's easy to get into a rut where you have acquired many bad habits. Staying up too late, not eating properly, and being unable to tell someone "no," can all lead to a gamut of ailments that include headaches, illnesses, and poor performance.

Therefore, you must learn how to train your mind, body, and soul in a way that is beneficial. The results from taking matters into your own hands must lead to positive outcomes and renewed strength to manage the depth and workload of your small business.

Take a minute to evaluate yourself and to make sure that you are not the problem that is preventing future progress. Be honest with yourself. As my mother always told me, "Regina, you don't get enough rest," and "You've got too many people to pay." Then I would listen intently, purge my mind, evaluate my staff, change my attitude, stop, inhale, exhale, believe again, and keep moving forward. After that, I would take her advice and, "Get some rest."

A healthy, peaceful mindset will help you stay in business for many years to come. Make it a point to be intentional and on purpose; create a powerful strategy for success and make it happen. The business and its future are depending on you.

Chapter 11

MEET NEW CHALLENGES HEAD-ON

THE DRIVING FORCE BEHIND the entrepreneur who wants to stay in business can be an awesome source of magical power. It is like an internal, unseen, spiritual, driving force that is immediately activated by some new, seemingly hard challenge that needs to be faced and conquered. I call them "unforeseen opportunities" that can become a great source of additional revenue, depending upon how you examine the possibilities and determine your potential. It may be possible, but do you have the potential and drive to carry out the duties, thereby achieving the task?

These new challenges should be met head-on with zeal and authority. Sometimes, you just have to "act" like you know what you're doing. Speak with power and talk like you know how to do it. Question anyone else's ability to carry out the task and present the facts that show you're knowledgeable about the subject matter.

Make it a point to demonstrate a winning attitude as you say to yourself, "Yes, I can do this." Yes, we can handle it! Garner the wherewithal to "hang tough" in "tough situations." Believe in yourself and your goals. Smile often and make the attempt to do more.

For example, in the very early stages of my business back in 1985, I approached the campaign manager of Tom Barrow, who had announced that he would run for Mayor of the City of Detroit. I telephoned their headquarters and asked him if our business could submit samples of t-shirts and be hired as a vendor providing merchandise for the upcoming campaign. I was invited to meet with him and his campaign manager in their office. I picked up their campaign logo/design and told them that I would deliver the sample t-shirts in two weeks. I had the zeal. I was bold and confident that we could perform the task. I had the faith!

Mind you, at this stage of my business, we didn't have *any* printing equipment, no building, no t-shirt distributor contacts, no suppliers, and no store location. All I had were the guts to proceed forward, based upon my "profitable experience" with t-shirt sales that went through the roof during the 1984 World Series when the Detroit Tigers became the World Champions! That was such a great, eye-opening event!

Always think big. Think beyond your wildest dreams! Think beyond your biggest goal. Beyond your greatest expectations! Think beyond your best accomplishment! At the time, I did not know much about printing, or providing merchandise in the political arena. I was not aware of any special procedure for handling campaign contracts, and I had no experience as a Union printing facility.

However, I did know that if I landed the account, and worked a good deal, and sufficiently met the challenge, it would provide a great source of revenue for several months throughout the election process. Until Election Day, win or lose, my small business would benefit financially and gain publicity, whether or not Tom Barrow would obtain enough political support and votes to dethrone the Honorable Mayor Coleman A. Young.

It was such an exciting time in the City of Detroit! I was so delighted about the task, because this was a great opportunity with immense potential, and I believed that we had the capacity to carry it out. I kept thinking and saying to myself, "This job can lead to other politicians hiring us to print for their campaigns and events."

Two weeks later, I delivered the samples to Tom Barrow's campaign office. They were pleased and commended our timeliness and professionalism. Meanwhile, I had found and hired another local silk-screen printer to expedite the job! A little hard work can go a long way with diligence and persistence.

Yet in spite of our efforts, another vendor was chosen and hired to provide them with the campaign merchandise. Of course, Mayor Young remained in his position for another term from 1985 until 1989. He was unbeatable! And a great man for an incredible time in history.

In 1993, two new candidates emerged onto the scene to run for the illustrious position of Mayor of the City of Detroit: former Michigan Supreme Court Justice Dennis W. Archer and Sharon McPhail. Both were well-known attorneys throughout the community. As a result of our efforts, we were able to capitalize from our early experience with political campaigns. We wound up providing merchandise for both political candidates.

I landed the account with the Archer campaign after attending a public Town Hall meeting. When they took questions from the audience, my dear cousin nudged me and said, "Ask him about his commitment to small businesses!" After the meeting, one of his assistants approached me to get my business card, which led us to provide products and services for his campaign. A few weeks later, we were contacted to provide items for the opposing candidate, Sharon McPhail. For us, it was a win-win situation. Our story was featured in *Crain's Detroit Business* in 1996 in an article written by Jeffrey McCracken. We were celebrating our 10th Anniversary at the time.

As you travel the business journey of remaining successful, you will have to navigate many high and low periods. At any rate, these periods can be conceived as great opportunities to boldly step into new challenges with excitement, authority, and a spark of new energy to attempt a different approach. It's all about expanding and stabilizing your business methods that will bring forth new ideas and greater profits.

Don't run from these challenges, because timing is very important. The situation might be exactly what you need for that moment in time. Stand firm. Pull your thoughts together. Evaluate the extreme benefits of the impending decision and go with an option. Winning is always available. Winners never give up, never give in, and never give out, because there's always a better way. To stay in business, you must be willing to tap into your resources and find a better way. It's always there.

Special Note: I started the outline for this writing in March of 2006, after we celebrated our 20th Anniversary. The new challenge for us was completing the expansion of our new printing/retail facility, officially creating our new World Headquarters. I will share the outcome of this challenge in my final chapter.

Chapter 12

GIVE PEOPLE A CHANCE AND GO FURTHER

"A lot of people can do things, if they were only given the chance."

Regina DuBose
as quoted in *The Detroit Free Press*

IN 1993, *THE DETROIT Free Press* quoted me in a front-page article about small businesses that were providing goods and services for the Inaugural Celebrations for incoming Detroit Mayor Dennis Archer.

"A lot of people can do things, if they were only given the chance," I was quoted as saying in the newspaper. At that time, The Alexis Company was hired to provide more than 3,000 balloons and decorations for three of the 13 Inaugural parties that were scheduled for the newly elected Mayor. This was a definite milestone and excellent boost for our small business efforts and staying power. I really didn't know how "big" this opportunity was until much later!

Whenever you give other people a chance, you will discover so many hidden talents of the individuals who surround you. This includes your staff, customers, business friends, key supporters, and family members. You may hire someone to handle the position of cashier and later discover that they possess artistic skills, and that they are a good fit to strengthen the creative logistics in your business. They may assist with the visual layout of your store's merchandise or graphic designs and sign making. It's a strange phenomenon, but I believe it is true when guidance counselors express that most people maintain a vocation—the job which earns their living—and an avocation—the job they love to do "on the side."

Somewhere along the line, you have to learn to trust the abilities of others who have the capacity to make your business life simpler and more effective. Believe that they can handle the details and the responsibilities. Allow them to follow through on an assignment. Believe that they have the right skills needed to advance your goals. You must believe in your decision to give other people a chance, and then live with the consequences and results. For better or worse, the outcome can be a great avenue for growth and change, helping you to stay in business. Other people have so much to offer. Just ask.

Along the road of building business success, I made some mistakes with giving other people a chance, but I grew tremendously from those errors and became more certain and confident about my business pursuits. I guess my professional background as a guidance counselor, along with previous work in the community mental health field, as well as growing up in a household where my youngest brother was physically handicapped, all made me susceptible and open to hiring "others." This is the classification placed on people who are rarely given a second chance to work in a good, decent employment setting. They may have special needs and concerns that have kept them afraid or isolated from the world of work. At The Alexis Company, we stretched to provide an atmosphere of acceptance to all.

Over the years, we have hired persons who were laid-off from the factory, along with former substance abusers, recovering alcoholics, slow learners eager to show their skills, disadvantaged students, those who were physically handicapped, and individuals who often felt that mainstream society had given up on them. One of my favorite staff members for at least five to six years was an elderly gentleman who lived near our store location. He would faithfully stop by on a weekly basis, to beg for cash to support his drinking habit.

One day, I asked him to sweep in front of our building in exchange for some money. Payment for services seemed more feasible from my position and past experiences, rather than just giving a free handout for an obviously bad habit. He agreed to the arrangement and came by weekly to sweep in front of the store, take out the garbage, shovel snow during the winter months, and clean up the trash that accumulated around the City of Detroit bus stop that was conveniently situated in front of our store.

He was pleased to receive the monetary gifts that we gave him and felt a strong connection to our business, in a meaningful way. I learned that when you go out of your way to accept people as they are, with their own issues, you will find creative ways to help them. And when you give them a chance, they will demonstrate a desire to help you. I often told my staff to treat everyone who comes through the door with "dignity and respect," no matter what condition they appeared to exhibit. This included the least respected individual to the highly recognized corporate executive who was visiting our store. I am a firm believer in human potential and capacity.

Everybody is important. And every human being is somebody special to someone. Every person has something positive to offer. We just need to acknowledge it. When you develop the mentality to take the risk and give people a fair chance, your business will flourish without limitations. You increase the chances of staying in business longer.

Finally, give yourself a chance! Give yourself a chance to do the necessary evaluation that is important and significant to determine if owning a small business is the absolute best route for you. Ask yourself, "Is this what will make me happy? Do I feel like I'm on a successful track? Do I have the capacity to finish the work involved to make this business a profitable venture?"

Many people have the potential to do well in small business, but they lack the capacity. I have found that both components are mandatory to start, own, run, and remain in small business. It is definitely a major journey. And I strongly believe that it is so important to know oneself. I am convinced that each manager has a set of strengths and weaknesses. As you maximize your ability, build upon your strengths, and manage your weaknesses, success is inevitable, and longevity becomes achievable. Just watch your business reach its projected goals and full potential. When that happens, you will maximize your growth.

Potential is the presented possibilities that are readily available to a willing person who has a set of skills. **Capacity** is the amount of depth given to an individual that allows him or her to get the most volume out of their given skill set.

For instance, you might be a good automotive mechanic or an attorney, but that doesn't necessarily mean you can handle the responsibilities of running an auto repair shop or managing a real estate law firm. The potential or opportunity is where this may be possible. However, the skills necessary to be an effective business owner are not automatically transferrable, but based on the capacity of that individual. Be honest with yourself. Most self-help authors will encourage you to look at your strengths and weaknesses. I suggest that you should carefully examine your ability, potential, and capacity. In the business game, so many people quit and give up early. They end up missing out on their hopes and dreams, settling for less.

Give yourself a chance to make mistakes, learn from them, and move to a new sense of understanding. Add to your own ideas by sharing your thoughts and business objectives with those who can assist and support you. Learn to cope with the reality of your business situation and explore different techniques to move past your obstacles. **You can** overcome any deficiency.

I remember worrying about taking care of my elderly mother (my father died in June 1992) and trying to organize the daily operations at my store. Eventually, I figured it out and decided to pick her up at lunch time and bring her to the store to enjoy as well as participate.

In 2003, when she turned 75 years old (three-quarters of a century!), I was thrilled to give her a surprise birthday party! Later that night, when all the festivities had settled down, she told me, "I am officially retired and not working anymore!" With all due respect, I replied, "Amen, Momma." Also, don't be afraid to ask for help! That is not a weakness. It is a great measure of your needs and level of satisfaction. Keep looking for the right combinations that can take your business to a whole new level.

Explore your options as you constantly re-work your business plan of action. If you notice, I have not said much about the importance of your business plan throughout this book. That precious written document tells and foretells the strategic map and pathway, entailing the goals you plan to pursue and accomplish as you operate a successful, small enterprise. That's because, as you now know from my story, I didn't start my business with a business plan!

In fact, we generated a business plan after several years of running our company. And it grew from our need to obtain money to stay in business! Here's what happened. I sent an update letter to close friends and family members, asking them to donate $100 to our cause. It was in 1989, and we were in desperate need of funds to order new inventory, pay our suppliers, purchase some equipment, and cover some overhead expenditures. It was the first time I actually sat down and began to process what we were doing, where we were heading, and how to lay out our future plans. My "potential donors" were asking for a specific business plan, and rightfully so. It's business!

As you know, we created our business in my parents' basement during June and July of 1984, and moved into the actual store location on March 16, 1986. By 1989, we were becoming a full-fledged, daily operation. We were open to the general public Monday through Saturday from 9:00 a.m. until 6:00 p.m., and on Sundays by appointment only. On many occasions, we made special deliveries to satisfy weekend parties and celebrations. As I examined the need to re-organize, I began to realize and accept that a business plan, clearly written, was the exact tool that would provide the necessary direction to move forward, ascend to the next level, and stay in business longer.

We were successful in getting positive responses and raised enough funds to satisfy our initial financial goals. As a result of that action, I learned the power of OPM (Other People's Money): money that was acquired, but did not come from a bank, financial institution, or personal loan. This was a better approach to raising funds and led to years of support, stability, and satisfaction.

Before I close and end this writing, let me quickly share what happened to our "World Headquarters." The reality of the global economy was the name of the game. In 2006, we celebrated our 20th year in business. I had acquired a lease for a huge facility with great ideas, a new marketing plan, a strategy to capitalize on the economy, the use of internet services, and a training program for new staff.

However, from 2007 until 2017, I experienced the personal removal of key people in my life through a series of: deaths (family/friends); the abrupt, uneven retirement of educators (buyouts); the financial/housing and political crisis; the lack of contractors to remodel; and an unsettling in my stomach due to conflict at my religious setting (church and place of stability). After those experiences, I moved out of the building in May of 2018. However, I decided to stay in business and plan my exit strategy. I focused on perpetuating the wealth that I have accumulated, and on writing my books.

The purpose of this book is to serve as a brief digest summarizing some of the methods and techniques that were used to build, sustain, and expand our small business. My goal was to share some insight, provide guidance, open your mind, and encourage you to stand firm while pursuing your objectives as an entrepreneur. We have provided some snapshots, hoping to give you a vivid display of our journey. We traveled from destination to destination in business, relationships, management, and future outlook. I shared my secrets for success.

Thank you for reading this material. Remember, the longer you stay in business, the more you gain the ability to control your destiny, live your dreams, and have a fulfilling life. I've learned so much from Robert Kiyosaki, whom I met years ago at the Jacob Javits Convention Center in New York City. I admire him so much, I feel inspired to end with one of his quotes:

"It's more important to grow your income than cut your expenses. It's more important to grow your spirit than cut your dreams."[4]

May you start, grow, maintain, and stay in business for a long time.

Be Peaceful and God Bless You,

Regina A. DuBose

Author Bio

REGINA DUBOSE WAS BORN in Detroit, Michigan in 1957. She was educated in the Detroit Public School system and was raised in a loving family with her parents and four brothers.

Ever since her first lemonade stand as a kid, Regina DuBose was drawn to entrepreneurship. However, it was her first job as a clerk-typist for a reputable accounting firm, Thompson and Edwards CPAs in Detroit, which opened the door for Regina to receive true mentorship from a successful entrepreneur. That experience increased Regina's financial IQ and taught her some basics about interacting with clients, as well as money management and tax law. She has continued to incorporate these lessons throughout her life and career. As the youngest employee at the firm and the only African American, she was already a trailblazer and has made creating opportunities for others a major part of her life's mission and work.

Regina received a Bachelor of Arts degree in Psychology, and a Master of Arts degree in Guidance and Counseling, from Wayne State University, with continued graduate studies at Rutgers University. For 13 years, she practiced as a counselor in the field of educational psychology, until turning her sights back to her first love and pursuing her dream of being a business owner.

In 1984, she began small as a vendor at concerts, local festivals, and events, selling novelty items and inflatable toys. By 1986, she'd saved enough to open The Alexis Company. Through trial and error, Regina quickly adapted in the business world, expanding her product line over time to include party supplies, balloons, and party décor, along with gift items, and finally what became her signature product, silk-screened t-shirts.

For 35 years, The Alexis Company has thrived as a community staple serving major churches, schools, and community organizations, as well as high-profile clientele, including former Detroit Mayor Dennis Archer, Fifth-Third Bank, and Senator Hansen Clark.

She is a member of the Advertising Specialty Institute, the Detroit Metropolitan Visitors & Convention Bureau, and Motor City Freedom Riders. An avid community activist and person of faith, Regina volunteers regularly and serves as a member of the Midwest Civic Council of Block Clubs, and the New Members Teacher at Partakers Church Baptist. She shares her life with her daughter, Dr. Sequina DuBose, who is a classical musician, opera singer, and college professor. Regina loves to travel, cook, sing, and play board games to relax.

With *Perpetuating Wealth*, Regina aspires to continue in the footsteps of her first financial mentors and encourage others to pursue their entrepreneurial dreams.

Acknowledgments

WHEN I THINK ABOUT 35 years of operating a small business, there are so many people to thank. Let me first start with God, the Creator of the Universe, who gave me the breath of life. And I thank my African Ancestors who made it across the Atlantic Ocean to America.

I thank Mary Lou Neal and William Felix Hinkle, my paternal grandparents who created the Hinkle family. I thank Bessie Moor and David Creag who were my maternal grandparents and created my mother Rosie Lee, who married Samuel Matthew Hinkle. I thank my loving parents for love and kindness. I thank my brothers Samuel M. Hinkle Jr. and James Allen Hinkle for your brilliance. I thank all of my aunts, uncles, and cousins who were around during my childhood upbringing. Thank you: Aunt Harrietta (Cousin Jr. Ruffin), Uncle Harry (Cousin Helen), Aunt Nancy and Uncle George Manuel (Cousin Victor), Aunt Littie Ann (who lived with us), Mary (Dear) Freeman and Uncle Sylvester, Mama Freeman, and Alexis Jane and Donald Hill (my first cousin whom I was named after). I thank Cousin Mary Catherine who owned a restaurant in Dayton, Ohio. I also thank Aunt Mary Cooper and Uncle Eddie (Cousin Billy Bo), Aunt Ruth (Toot) Miller and Uncle Rufus

(Rufus James), and Uncle Robert Lee Creag (who lived with us).

I thank: Cousin Mary Catherine Mason and Auntre DuBose, my mother and father-in-law who showed me love and kindness (Sequoia); James R. Thompson, CPA (my first boss) and Rev. Dr. Valmon D. Stotts; and Mrs. Dorothy Griffin and Mrs. Annie Ellis (Sunday school teachers) at Unity Baptist Church. It is with great appreciation and in loving memory that I acknowledge your presence in the early years of my life. You are truly missed, and I thank God for your contribution to my personal journey.

I thank Anita Owens (my first girlfriend) and the Floyd Street Block Club Family—the neighborhood where "every house had a name." I also thank my brother Ronnie and nephew Samuel III who stood by my side during the learning years of owning a business and doing everything that was necessary to help the business grow. I thank my neighbor's daughter Davita Davis who was my first employee. I thank my nephews Ronnie Jr. and Andre, and Steven Hinkle who worked diligently over the years. I thank my daughter Sequina, for promoting the business by letting people know, "My mother prints t-shirts!" Thank you to my niece, Santrice, who blew up balloons when she was five years old. Thank you, Janice Robinson, for your unique face painting at our events.

I thank all of my relatives, young people, neighbors, church members, students, and friends who supported the efforts to make the business a huge success. I thank my best friends from high school: Mrs. Yasmin Atkins and Dr. Pamela Bradford; Carolyn and Jaunice Flowers; Joyce Keener and the Super Bowl Clan; Janice, Vincent, and the Goree family; as well as Nina R. Scott and Patrice DeBose (Renaissance High School Varsity Chorus). I thank Marlene

Archey Crim, Esq. for your words of wisdom. Thank you, Dr. Irma Hamilton, teachers, and educators. I thank my partner, graphics designer, and friend Mr. Arthur Williams and his wife Shanell; and Mary Johnson Grant (Cousin Mae Mae) for pushing me forward to reach my goals. I thank my first cousins Floyd Johnson and Gloria Jean Wesson for their love and encouragement.

I thank the Trios of older women (Titus 2:3-5) who were my role models: Zeborah Hampton Hardy, Denise Livingston Dryden and Shelley Peters Davis (neighbors); Vernice Miller, Dr. Shelley McIntosh, and Jacqueline Miller (first cousins on my mother's side); Jewel Jones, Nancy Mayes (entrepreneur extraordinaire), and Mary Johnson Grant (first cousins on my father's side); and Mrs. Rose Harvey, Mrs. Elizabeth Davis and Mrs. Sarah Jenkins (great church soloists). I thank Dr. Dorgan J. Needom, Minister of Music, and Mrs. Eunice Wade for being my friend, music composer/arranger, and personal accompanist at Unity Baptist Church.

I sincerely thank Mrs. Jacquetta Crews, my sixth-grade teacher who also taught my daughter, and all the great teachers who were at Hanneman Elementary School. Thank all of you for your special role in the development of my character, leadership, strength, courage, and fortitude as a woman and small business owner.

Finally, there are friends and colleagues who made this dream a reality. I want to first of all, thank all of the Silk Screen Printers and small business owners who came to my rescue and assisted my quest in business: Mr. Chester Vaughn of Blackness Unlimited; Mr. Reggie Lester of B & B Tee Shirt Factory; Mr. J. Michael of Jam Enterprises; and Mr. Charles Kimball (the Poster Man). I thank Mr. Mike of Zakoor's Novelty; Mr. Jeffery Turner (Special Events

Vendor); Mr. Howard Blackmon (Major Sports Vendor); Mr. George and Jose Tanifum (Cameroon, West Africa family); and my partner abroad, Mr. Rudolph Emange.

I thank my photographer, Mr. E. Donald Sherman. I thank Mr. Thomas Grenfell, President of Detroit Typographical Union #18, for keeping our business on course. I thank Mr. Gary Winston, Dr. Fayyaz Zahid (visionary leadership), and Mr. Shahbaz Hussein of Liberty Tax Service for their collaborative effort. And I thank all of the suppliers and distributors who provided merchandise and products to support our customer base and business goals.

Next, I thank Mr. James R. Thompson, Mr. Rick and Ann Edwards, Mrs. Sophie and Dan Konchak, and Mrs. Janet and Russell Halleen, for the lessons learned and opportunity at Thompson & Edwards, CPAs.

I also thank Ms. Linda Moragne and Mr. Steve Holsey of *The Michigan Chronicle*. I thank the media personalities who supported my business via newspaper articles, weekly magazines, and radio coverage.

I thank my customers for your love, encouragement, patronage, kindness, and support. The list includes the many churches, schools, groups, block clubs, associations, politicians, city officials, teachers, principals, nonprofits, bazaars, festivals, conferences, family reunions, seminars, workshops, and small businesses, and anyone whom I have not mentioned or acknowledged. You are all appreciated very much.

Finally, I thank my committee who surrounded me with understanding, cooperation, and participation to support this project. I express sincere gratitude and respect for Dr. DaNita Weddle for reading, editing, and guiding the expressions of my writing for grammar and clarity. Your brilliance helped to paint the complete picture. I thank Rev. Dr. Lee C. and Kimberly Winfrey for your prayers, preaching, and teaching at Partakers Church Baptist; you provided the environment to grow spiritually and to dream, again. Your words provoked me to open the drawer filled with my old, scraggly notes and outline to finish writing this book.

I thank Eric J. Bowren, CPA of Edwards, Ellis & Associates, P.C., for financial intelligence, administration, and consultation. I thank Dr. Sequina DuBose and Mr. Ajani Winston for technical genius, graphic design, and personal assistance. I thank my mentor, Dr. Glenda Price, who steered me in the right direction with wisdom, knowledge, and inspiration. Thank you for embracing my vision.

I thank Dan and Darlene Swanson, as well as Mr. Bobby Ivory, Jr., for navigating the graphics of this project. Thank you, Sheri Burton, President of Midwest Civic Council of Block Clubs, for believing and compelling me to walk; I can now run. Thank you, Robert Quinn Hampton, for your sincere dedication and commitment.

Lastly, by the Grace of God and His infinite power, I thank the dynamic publishing team of Elizabeth Ann Atkins and her sister, Catherine M. Greenspan, of Two Sisters Writing and Publishing for taking on this project and creating the magical space to fulfill my dream. Your approach to coaching, leading, publishing, and fostering great authors is impeccable. Thank you for the consultation, supervision, and explanation for everything throughout the process. I am grateful for your knowledge, enthusiasm, standards of excellence, experience, and expertise. You are amazing!

I personally thank Judge Marylin E. Atkins for walking into

my store many years ago to order some ink pens, and the Sovereign Will of God that prevails in my life.

Thank You So Much,
Regina Alexis DuBose

Bibliography

THE FOLLOWING BOOKS ARE recommended for you to improve your chances of staying in business. They present information on expanding your financial intelligence, increasing wealth, and developing a mindset that will promote your ability to manage the responsibilities of an Entrepreneur.

Lowell Lundstrom, *How You Can Enjoy Super-Natural Prosperity*, (Eugene, OR: Harvest House Publishers, 1979).

Thomas J. Stanley, Ph.D. and William D. Danko, *The Millionaire Next Door,* (New York: Gallery Books, 1996).

Thomas J. Stanley, Ph.D., *The Millionaire Mind,* (Kansas, MO: Andrews McMeel Publishing, 2000).

Michael Pink, *The Bible Incorporated,* (Cleveland, OH; New York City: World Publishing, 1988).

Florence Scovel Shinn, *The Wisdom of Florence Scovel Shinn*, (Wichita, KS: Fireside Publishing, 1989).

Robert T. Kiyosaki with Sharon L. Lechter, C.P.A., *Rich Dad, Poor Dad* (New York: Warner Books, 1997).

Robert T. Kiyosaki, *CashFlow Quadrant, Rich Dad's Guide to Financial*

Freedom (New York: Warner Books, 1998).

Robert T. Kiyosaki with Sharon L. Lechter, C.P.A., *Rich Dad's Guide to Investing*, (New York: Warner Books, 2000).

C. I. Scofield, D. D., *The New Scofield Study Bible, Holy Bible*, Authorized King James Version, (New York: Oxford University Press, 1967). Specifically, The Entire Book of Proverbs; Proverbs 22:7; 1 Timothy 6:6-12; Ecclesiastes 2:24; 10:19; 12:1, 13-14; Psalms 1:1-3; and Joshua 1:8-9.

Endnotes

1   Robert Kiyosaki and Sharon Lechter, C.P.A., *CASHFLOW Quadrant: Rich Dad's Guide to Financial Freedom* (Scottsdale, AZ: Plata Publishing, 2011). https://www.amazon.com/Rich-Dads-CASHFLOW-Quadrant-Financial-ebook/dp/B0175P5MZU Accessed 9-17-21.

2   Robert T. Kiyosaki with Sharon L. Lechter, C.P.A., *Rich Dad, Poor Dad* (New York: Warner Books, 1997). https://www.amazon.com/Rich-Dad-Poor-Money-That-Middle/dp/0446677450. Accessed 9-17-21.

3   Merriam-Webster Dictionary, Merriam-Webster.com, https://www.merriam-webster.com/dictionary/train. Accessed 9-4-21.

4   Robert T. Kiyosaki, Facebook.com, November 3, 2017, https://www.facebook.com/33416011787/posts/its-more-important-to-grow-your-income-than-cut-your-expenses-its-more-impor-tant/10155772013961788/. Accessed 9-4-21.

CPSIA information can be obtained
at www.ICGtesting.com
Printed in the USA
BVHW020222171221
624254BV00001B/4

* 9 7 8 1 9 4 5 8 7 5 8 3 0 *